Sept 15, 2010

Dearly Georgeanne,

Thank you for purchasing this book,
Thank you also for your presence
at my book launch.

Jackie's love and beauty connected
you and me. Knowing your family is
being at home in America.

I love you with all the Woman In Me.

Thank you for letting me be
part of your family.

Ng. Udoye — Jackie's Care-giver
(Mama Sophia)

THE WOMAN IN ME

The Struggles of an African Woman to Discover Her Identity and Authority

Mama Sophia

authorHOUSE®

AuthorHouse™
1663 Liberty Drive
Bloomington, IN 47403
www.authorhouse.com
Phone: 1-800-839-8640

First published by AuthorHouse   9/1/2010

ISBN: 978-1-4520-4616-7 (sc)
ISBN: 978-1-4520-4617-4 (hc)
ISBN: 978-1-4520-4615-0 (e)

Library of Congress Control Number: 2010909709

Printed in the United States of America
Bloomington, Indiana

This book is printed on acid-free paper.

CONTENTS

ACKNOWLEDGMENTS

Special thanks to the following readers for their sincere and effortful participation in the initial proofreading: Anne Ream, Rev. Fr. Bill Zimmer, Mary Toman, Blessing Borha, Rev. Deacon George Borha, Peggy Delaney, Mary Riel, Prof. Ron Morgan.

INTRODUCTION

Whether rich or poor, female or male; powerful or weak; white, black, or brown; child or adult, there are some things we all yearn for that money cannot buy. We all long for peace. We search for happiness wherever we think it can be found. We all want to love and be loved. We long for freedom. We expect that our human dignity will be respected. This dignity is strongly tied to our *within* authority bequeathed to us—woman or man—at creation. It is an identity we all carry.

The human person is endowed with a built-in authority. This authority empowers us to fly. Yes, we can fly! My identity was formed when I learned I was an eagle and not a chicken. My authority emerged when I learned how to fly. If you have been knocked off your feet more often than usual, you should know how to fly. Learning how to fly is part of what being human means. I learned how to fly from hammer blows of experience.

Finally, I have learned that happiness is not outside of us. It is within us, waiting to be discovered. This awareness is liberating and empowering.

Arts are African Women's ways of telling their stories through songs, dance, storytelling, writing, painting, weaving, etc. My goals in this project are twofold: first to tell my own story, and secondly to communicate to the world the experiences and stories of the voiceless African women and their children. This first book is an introduction to five-year, ongoing research called *African Women and the Psychology of Oppression*. The contents are mostly my story, beliefs, and philosophies, as well as experiences shared by many African women. Some of their stories are breathtaking; some are heartbreaking.

As the president of African Women in America (AfWiAm), working with the women while traveling extensively to more than twenty-seven African countries has revealed how similar their experiences are. The cultural victimization and oppression of African women seems to follow a pattern.

Women and gender is fast-becoming a global field of study. Very often I feel the African woman is still excluded from global academic and social justice efforts. This book is an effort to fill that gap. Also, with this book in hand, I hope to begin scheduling and accepting appearances for presentations, talks, and public speaking. I hope to use television shows, radio, Internet, and any other media outlets that can get the attention of young African and American women. My targets are AfWiAm members, American women groups, students (especially female), rural and urban African women in Africa, African women who are first and second generation Americans, women's groups and organizations, and other interested persons and/or groups who wish to learn about the African woman.

Naming is a powerful ritual in African culture. Names are symbolic phenomena. When you name someone or something, you have control over her, him, or it. Hence Africans have attributory names for God, which emanate from relational experiences with God. Descriptive names for the Supreme Being may originate from their beliefs in what the Creator does in their lives. Throughout this book, different African attributes for the Supreme Being were used. The English letters do not contain some of the original alphabets used in these names. Therefore, some moderations have been made to accommodate the spellings. My sincere apologies to the cultures affected.

The following are the different African names for GOD some of which were used throughout this book.

ZAMBE in Congo; NYIKOB, MBOO, SIYINI in Cameroon; OMUTONZI, KATONDA, MLUNGU, NYASAYI, WERE in Kenya; MUNGU in Swahili; MAWU in Togo and Ghana; ONYAME, EWURADE in Ghana; RUHANGA in Tanzania; KABUMBA-WESU, LESA, CHIFWE in Zambia; EGVIBHAIR, WAAKA in Ethiopia; OCHAMACHALA, CHUKWU, DINWENUM, CHINEKE, OLUWA, OLORUN, OLISAH, OGHENE in Nigeria; BAMBAM the Almighty, is mine, developed from personal experiences with the Supreme Being.

This book is dedicated to the Blessed Virgin Mary Mother of Jesus on whose lap Jesus was schooled as he struggled to discover his identity and authority. This work was made possible through her intercession.

I also dedicate this book to my mother, Mary Ann Udoye. It was she who taught me that I was born an eagle and not a chicken. She was the woman who taught me to hold on to my authority.

This is also for all the African women whose lives have touched and shaped me.

Finally, I want to honor all the African children whose love powered my courage and necessitated this book.

CHAPTER ONE
Awareness

It was cool evening. A gentle breeze was blowing. The weather was so cool—it could have been 70 degrees. My compound—in fact, the entire village—was beautifully peaceful. Mother Nature could have been one of the sleeping beauties at this hour. The sounds of insects, birds, goats, sheep, and other creatures orchestrated a harmony that predisposed the afternoon as being evil free. So I thought.

It was our market day, and most of the adult members had gone to the market. On market days, it is common to see the very young and the very old home alone. My cousins Matthew and Angela were living with us at the time. They were in the backyard preparing palm nuts. Samuel, one of the notorious boys from my village, entered my father's compound (In 2000 when I started my personal life search, I found out that Samuel could have been 10 – 12 years older than me). Honestly speaking I do not remember how old I was, but that experience drew an indelible mark on my memory. I ran out to see who was at the gate. I could have been no more than four or five years, but age is not as important as the experience. At that age, I was a very curious child; maybe more inquisitive than a monkey.

I regret that day—the day my inquisitive nature was crushed. Samuel picked me up and sat me on the front porch rail. I wanted to scream but was too scared. He held me on the rail with one hand and started to unzip his trousers with the other hand. I sensed evil was looming. I suspected he was going to do something bad when he started to unzip his trousers in my presence. At first I looked into his eyes, as if to remind him that what he was about to do was sinful. My religion had taught me that boys and girls should not do improper things such as I suspected Samuel was about to do. The look from his eyes was more mean than human. I started to cry, pleading,"Please! No! Please! No!" He raped me. I could not help but let out a loud cry. He quickly let me down and pulled up his trousers. By the time my cousins came to the scene, I had already run into the house and hid under my father's bed. I could hear him say, "I didn't do anything." I became more frightened when I heard him lie. Immediately, I started to blame myself, "I should have run away. I should have yelled as loud as my voice could carry". It was my fault," I whispered to myself. I was so scared and frightened. I started to shake. I must have passed out because by the time I woke my mother was sitting beside me on her bed. She asked me what happened. I said, "Nothing." She pressed and I insisted there was nothing. I became ill for the rest of the week, too scared to be left alone. From that day, my mom did not allow me to be home alone until I was old enough to defend myself.

I am an African woman. My growing up is not that great a story. During my girlhood and adolescence, I was a weakling. I was a timid and extremely shy adolescent. Like many traditional African women, I started out feeble and fragile. Now people look at me and see a strong African woman. I am full of energy and highly motivated. "She is rarely angry," they say. They perceive me as always being happy. They think it would take great evil to break me. Many of my colleagues admire my calm, serene aura. Some think it is not natural. However, I know it is. I have stopped trying to explain because I do not explain well. The source of my serenity is deep within. The secret is prayer. My staff of authority is love. My joy is deep-rooted and indescribable. I have not always been in touch with this *me,* but I believe it has been there from the beginning. I only needed to discover it. I did not fight for it. All I did was tap into the source and there it was–where it has always been.

Who I am is stronger than what you see. It is immortal. The image and likeness of CHINEKE— the unknown, infinitely powerful, indefinable supreme deity who encompasses everything—in us is indestructible. That was why I could not be maimed by those cultural injustices, abuses, and victimizations. Those long-standing cultural practices are too many to count and too complex to explicate. Now I am liberated and free. To understand who I am is the highest freedom. To strive to live out who I am is the optimum liberty. I have discovered my authority. But I am not alone. I still think of my African mothers, sisters, and daughters. I do not forget those who may still be in shackles. I am determined to stand by them until they too are liberated. As long as they are still in chains, I am not yet free.

When experience becomes overwhelming, reasoning goes on break, and we become speechless. The pen dries up and writing becomes impossible. That was my situation for a very long time. And that is still the situation of many African women and children. It was difficult to be logical about subjective experiences. I was so immersed in the "pot" of injustice, dehumanization, degrading abuse, and victimization that I could not be analytical about my situation. The culture was and in many cases still is unjust toward women and children. Conversely, it is even more difficult to be objective about something that one has no commensurate knowledge of or experience with. If you have not experienced it, you might not be able to understand it. I hope this essay will help you journey with me so that we can join hands in the liberation mission for African women.

Learning MySelf: Have you experienced suffering? Do you know someone who is going through unbearable pain as a result of loss, neglect, or abuse? Are you or is someone you know beginning to believe an ugly situation will not go away? Are you struggling financially? Do you feel financially secure but think something is missing? Do you ever feel like no one understands you or your situation? Have you felt like you should write a book about your life and the experiences you have had? Are you an African woman—or maybe any woman? The following tribute is for *you*. It comes from the bottom of my heart.

It is the tribute that empowers me to liberation. It reminds me who I am. It is this tribute that shapes my belief for myself, and not others' belief for me. From the moment I heard it whispered in my ear on behalf of African women, I became healed, strong, beautiful, and bold. I have discovered my authority, and my wings have developed and are strong. From that moment, I understood I am an eagle, not a chicken. For many years I was callow but now I know I can fly. And since then I have been flying. The sky is no longer my limit. My sky is the limit. And I will continue to soar until death, when I will be united with my Maker, never to be separated again.

If you accept this tribute and see yourself in this way, then rejoice and allow the Spirit to lead, direct, and empower you to the Creator's greater glory. If you do not see yourself in this tribute, work toward it. It is *you*, believe me! If you pay attention and pray, in time you will find out.

The Tribute: As a child of a virgin mind, she is born as a prodigy—a paragon of moderate giftedness. Blessing is embodied in her being as well as in what she will become. Even though she is a blessing, everywhere she goes it seems as if a curse follows her. The enemy knows who she is. Her life is a threat to the kingdom of darkness. But her defender is mighty, and her guide is wisdom. She learns who she is by looking into the eyes of others. She learns who she is through fears and struggles. Like every woman, her vocation to girlhood, womanhood, and motherhood is a gift as well as a calling. She has never known evil, but evil has haunted her for years—in her family, in the community, in the church, in school, everywhere she goes. Oftentimes the devil would sit on her shoulders and taunt her unceasingly. Her KABUMBA-WESU allowed it for the glory yet to be revealed. Occasionally, these taunts come in quick successions without a break. And it looks like it will never end. Like a mighty wind blowing high, which sometimes form tornadoes. These experiences bend her, but she is never broken. She is graced with pliancy. She bows in total surrender as the storm ragesand when it is quelled, she rises and stands tall because Mother Earth and Father Heaven stand by her.

The Great One is her teacher. She is schooled under the instructional master called hammer-blows of experience. Wisdom incarnate is her teacher. She becomes enlightened by the hardship that blinds many. Her tractability is beyond compare. She learns to run from the suffering that cripples many. She is a learner par excellence. She has allowed herself to be schooled by everything and everybody. Her other name is Sophia. To the great, a look into her eyes reveals a goddess. And when the lowly look into her eyes, they behold a compassionate mother. To her colleagues, she is an indomitable and amazing sister. She may look feeble but is puissant.

She has come to own her authority. She radiates power and love. Her identity is no longer hidden from the wise. Like many women, she has discovered her inner beauty and strength. Her outer self has been, like gold, tested by fire—except she is more precious than all the gold the world's money can buy. For the sake of the beauty that lies inside, her body was sent to hell. What she goes through is uncommon. This is so she can live. She lives to tell the story. She is only a voice. She is not the storier, nor does she claim to be the story. The storiers are the original owners of the experiences. She is only the storyteller. She is speaking because it is *time*. She can no longer keep silent.

She was born again and then again, three times. First she was a mother. Second, she was a midwife. Third, she was the baby. Each of these births was not without pains, agony, confusion, and cries. As a mother, she suffered through labor and birth pangs. As the newborn, she cried helplessly at birth. She cried for fear of the uncertainties of her new world, her culture, and new environment. She cried because she was forcefully ejected from the comfort of Mother Earth. As a newborn, she did not know that Mother Earth does not abandon any of her children. We live in her for a limited time before we are born. She prepares an eternal bed for our body after we die. Her welcome does not discriminate. High and low, men and women, children and adults, young and old, black and white, good and bad, righteous and sinners—everyone is welcome to sleep on the bed Mother Earth prepares for us when we die. A mother does not forget the child of her womb; even if she does, Father Heaven and Mother Earth do not.

As the midwife, her heart palpitated while she watched mother and child at the cauldron of death and life. Her heart trembled as she watched the separation process between mother and child, and she was happy to sever the umbilical cord. Gently, she put the newborn on the mother's bosom. Sweat and blood mixed to welcome the wonder child. The midwife donated her wrapper for covering. It became the newborn's swaddling cloth. At her birth, there was no gun salute. It was not a boy. If it was a prince, there would have been twenty one gun salute. It was a girl. But there was a cry. In the labor room we heard the cry. They were two persons but only one cry. Mother and child cried for the same purpose but for different reasons.

The Word Speaks*:* I have spoken. Yes! I spoke and you came into existence. I want you to speak as I did when My Word gave being and body to your matter and form. I want you to speak as I did when I spoke you into existence. I want you to speak as I taught you, my queen. For the sake of those whose daily lives are filled with drudgery, and for all the injustices they must face, I want you to speak, my love. Speak for those who suffer in silence because no one notices. You too have been there. Please do not forget, my Mother Earth. Arise, daughter! Arise, lovely sister! With you I can do a lot. Without me you can do nothing. I will always be by your side, whispering, prompting, reminding, admonishing, and encouraging. You shall live! All your daughters and sons as well! Freedom and beauty are your divine blessings! Authority is your birthright! Remember who you are! Claim your authority and everything else will fall into place. Rely on your second-chance spirituality. If you do not remember, never mind. Eventually, I will remind you about second-chance spirituality which will be discussed in the book *Mystery of a Call* (the diary of my spiritual journey). Remember, the mystery of your calling is when your future marries your past, and the power of the present is born into a wonderful energy. An energy that is loaded with authority and filled with peace, joy, freedom, equanimity, fruitfulness, wisdom, reverence, and indescribable beauty. Remember that the power of your authority is love. Please use it!

The Woman Responds: All these energies! Now I know that your gifts in us are not for keeping. I can't wait to share them with others. They are many and about to overwhelm me. I am ready for this dance. And I cannot stop dancing with you, my friend. I promise that all these energies will be channeled to developing KATONDA's trademark in all the children of the earth. This is our hope. We believe we can do it—you and me. This is our song! It is a song of love! We will sing it over and over—until the mission is accomplished. I urge you to begin to dance. At last, victory is ours. Let us dance!

Setting the Stage: I thought this, my first book about the African Woman, would present the findings from my ongoing research on her psychology of oppression. No! I cannot wait. That will be for the scholars; this book is for everybody, especially African women and girls. No matter how insignificant it may seem each of us needs to commence our individual participation in the liberation of African women.

Earth and heaven unite in their efforts to make the world the place our Mighty One intends for all the children of the world. We are all charged to make our world a better place. There should be no room for rancor and useless debate over who is important. Every age or group is important and has a contribution to make. Quite often I want to believe that the children and the elders are the most important groups, even though they do not represent the workforce. One of the models designed to take care of elderly women (the Golden Age Movement) holds that the elders are the custodians of traditions and culture. No society survives without the wisdom of its elders. Any generation that does not take good care of their elders wallows in darkness. If they neglect or abuse their elders, their women, or their children, they are in trouble. You may think they are vulnerable and maybe not as productive. But the truth is you can't do without them.

The world is a *universe*. Humans and all other created things form the unique rhyme in this verse that makes our world a beautiful music. If I may play on these words, I can say that the world is also a uni-*vase*. We all form a bouquet in this uni-*vase*. Different classes, races, ages, cultures, and ethnic groups make up the humanity of society and the functioning of it. Humanity is not made up of one class, one race, one age, one culture, or one ethnic group. The efficient functioning of any given society or culture depends on these different components being active participants in leadership and followership. It does not make sense for one group to think it is superior over another. As a matter of fact, it is a conscious violation of fundamental human rights when one class or group assumes perpetual dominance over another.

In African societies, the elders and children are supposed to be cared for by those who hold the batons of intergenerativity, the active adult members. There are two ends to a spectrum. I do not want to use the word *opposite*. The two ends are held together by the bar, or their life in between. Life is full of spectrums—heaven and earth, male and female, white and black, young and old, leader and follower, yesterday and tomorrow, past and future, and so on and so forth. For the most part, we fall into either end of a spectrum. The majority of us cannot be at both ends at the same time. At times, one might be at the bar in between. With this position comes enormous responsibility with respect to holding both ends of the spectrum.

CHAPTER TWO
Storytelling

***Living Story Life*:** On December 4, 2008, I had a short meeting with a small group of women at Loyola University Chicago's Gannon Center for Women in Leadership. There were three of us: Dawn Harris, PhD, the director of the center; Elizabeth Hemenway, PhD, the departmental chair of the Women's Studies program; and me. We attempted to articulate the role of history in the lives of human beings in general and, more importantly, in the lives of African women.

Loyola Women brainstorm with Mama Sophia (Elizabeth Hemenway, Ph.D; Dawn Harris, Ph.D., Ngozi Udoye, Ph.D)

In the evening, I reflected on the yields of the meeting. Reflecting on my day and life experiences is my way of taking stock. Taking stock helps me to do better the next day. I believe I make the same mistakes fewer times than I would have if I did not reflect. I am still a learner, and I make the same mistakes over and over. I am an active learner, but I am a slow one when it comes to living my personal life. That does not mean I am a dummy. That would be a false humility. Anyone who loves to learn cannot be dumb. As a matter of fact, I believe I am as sagacious as I can be when it comes to being an African woman. Furthermore, I do not believe I fit the stereotype many people have regarding the African woman.

For a time in the past, for more than three years, I made this the theme of my prayer: "Dear Omniscient Friend, give me the wisdom to discern your will and the courage to do it. For it is joy to know that I am spending this short life doing only that which pleases you." The Great Being heard my prayers and things have been different ever since. I have become a natural student. I am not saying that life has become simpler. The world is still full of mystery. If you peer deeper, you will see. You don't need to look—you need to see. The world's mysteries do not fit into any comprehensive theoretical framework. Hence, every experience has its own set of teaching contents and learning materials associated with it.

Many of us think we are fast learners. Some of us think we are smart. But the truth is the majority of us are neither fast learners nor smart. Challenge yourself by leaving your field of expertise, your comfort zone and personal context. Then you will better understand my argument. For example, we never realize how slow a learner we are until we critically reflect on our experiences or pray at the confessional every week or so. Oops! This may be the wrong example for some. Please tolerate my Catholicity here. I hope you will bear with me as I speak about my personal spirituality. Many people claim they no longer need this sacrament. I continue to practice the traditional sacrament of confession. Often times, I receive my healing at this sacrament. I recommend that we all participate in a disciplined life of regular confession or routine critical self-reflection. I believe confessions and therapy are related in many ways. Whether as a confessor, a therapist, or a counselor I need to have someone who is professionally trained before I can unload and unburden my innermost woes, weaknesses, and feelings, perhaps more so in this tense millennium than in any age and time of my life. When I can afford it, I let my money buy it at the counselor or psychologist's office. If not, I let my humility purchase it for free at the confessional. Either as a penitent or a client, I receive so much help from these.

I believe that my evening examination helps me reduce my naive mistakes. Grace collaborates with my desire to grow. In my religious community, this examination (St. Ignatius used the word *examen*) constitutes part of the spiritual exercises required of us. Reflections, daily examen, regular confession, and retreats are some of the components of "silence and solitude" discussed under "Secret of Her Strength" in Chapter 10. These exercises offer me the mirror with which I look into my heart and mind as well as my environment, all in relation to the Holy Other. With this mirror, I can make a better judgment as I struggle to ask: does this draw me closer to beauty, goodness, and greatness, or am I being drawn away from the beautiful image and likeness of our maker? Where does my authority lie in this case?

As I reflected on the women's meeting that evening, I thought, *Why did we spend thirty minutes talking about his story (history) when all we wanted to talk about was her story?* Story is said to be a woman's main way of sharing and learning, in contrast to man's. This is even more so for the African women. If a woman shares *her story* with you, she is inviting you into her world, her being, her time, and her space. She wants to enter into a dance with you. This dance must be a tango. It is not supposed to be a dance in which you are a spectator. It is a dance that is empowering, not belittling or pitying. If you are not ready to enter into a tango with an African woman, please do not ask her to share her story. You may be wounding what you intend to heal and may be disempowering those you wish to empower.

An African woman's story is usually about her experiences of struggles, dreams fulfilled, and dreams shattered. She is sharing her tears and laughter, her sorrows and joy. She is sharing her development and her obstacles, her strengths and weaknesses. An African woman is sharing the injustices and abuses meted out to her. The styles she uses may vary, but if you listen with your heart, you will hear what she wishes to communicate. *Her story* may be in a song or a dance. Mostly it is in her body and her voice, not just her words. When an African woman speaks *her story*, words alone usually do not adequately communicate what she wishes the world to know. So your attention must be trained to listen with your heart if you wish to hear what she is trying to communicate.

Her Being: The overall gist of what follows is a true story, although the names are fictitious. *Once upon a time, there lived in a beautiful town of Aricaf five damsels. Their names were Komma, Belle, Uzuri, Mma, and Beauty. When they were born, their beauty dazzled the elders so that the only name that befitted them was to call them what they are—Beauty. The five ladies received their names at their naming ceremony on the eighth day. They grew up true to their names—"onye abara-afa odi ya nu'kwe" (she embodies in her being what her name is). Their age-grade was the best in town. The entire people of Aricaf cherished them. Their beauty and wisdom were used to serve everyone they came in contact with. Aricaf* *was the most peaceful town in this part of the world. The town had great warriors and catlike wrestlers. None of their neighbors dared to confront them in tribal wars. Their women were admired and revered by all the neighboring towns and villages.*

Before long, war broke out among the neighboring clans of Aricaf. One of the clans felt the other clan was not obeying their ancestral treaty. They fought with clubs, bows, and arrows. It was supposed to be a war for the restoration of peace and justice, not a demonstration of might and wealth. The wars lasted for only two months because Aricaf intervened. To the natives and neighbors, however, it felt like the two clans had been fighting for twenty years. This was because they had known peace for many generations in the past.

During the war, women were protected and children were never harmed. Harming any woman or child of the warring parties would be considered an abomination that could incur the wrath of OCHAMACHALA. In fact, when any such war became fierce and unbearable to the citizens, women and children were used to stop the it. Women and children would be stationed in the frontlines of the battle. That was a request for peace to the other side. The town Aricaf used their women and children to request peace between the warring parties. They stationed their women in the battlefields in the night while the warring camps slept. Komma, Belle, Uzuri, Mma, and Beauty were among the women stationed at the front. The war ended the following morning when the warring parties saw the women and the children. They knew it was time-out. Disarmament was not difficult; the soldiers put down their clubs, bows, and arrows. Everyone went home to their respective clans and villages. Peace reigned again.

Peace had reigned for two days. Meanwhile, the civil government had dispatched its soldiers to the village of Aricaf. They arrived timely. But it was not they who quelled the violence but the peaceful presence of women and children, and not by clubs, bows, and arrows of the men and boys. But the soldiers thought their presence had brought the war to an end. The military dispatch did not want to leave. They stayed in the land with guns and sophisticated arms. The sound of their weapons made all the people and animals very uncomfortable. People were walking on eggshells. Many children developed hearing and mental disabilities from the shockwaves coming from the bullets and bombs. One of the boys born during this time was named Attii—shortened from artillery. Atti became hard of hearing from the explosions of heavy, sophisticated ammunitions.

One day, as Komma and Belle were going down to the stream, they were abducted by two of the government soldiers and raped. They wept so bitterly that no tears could flow. Instead blood flowed. They hugged as they buried their heads in each other's shoulders. They were filled with so much shame and guilt. They asked themselves and each other, "What did I do wrong? Why was I created a woman? We are very angry, but who will understand why? So we better clean up and go to fetch water for our families." They called out, "Uzuri! Mma! Beauty! Are you still home? Let's go, the sun will soon be out and the heat high." Uzuri, Mma, and Beauty answered from behind their mothers' respective huts. The five broke out into song as they walked like gazelles down to the river. Uzuri and Mma had been raped the previous day. They decided to conceal it from Beauty, Komma, and Belle. Beauty was the very first to be raped as soon as the soldiers arrived. Thanks to NYIKOB, who protects the innocent, none of them got pregnant. The five ladies lived with this heavy burden until they became mothers. Each of them told their story for the first time to their first daughter on the day she had her first menstruation. They all had a motive for telling this story to their daughters. Individually, they wanted to protect their own. That is why the five ladies told their daughters their rape stories. They surrounded their daughters with prayer, jealousy, vigilance, and the agility of a mother hen. They would do anything to protect their girls from human hawks.

Could they protect them? For how long? Usually a mother's protective strength does not last forever. Very soon, their girls would become women and would no longer be under their *mother hen's* protective, powerful wings. They must be severed from their mother's apron if they are to become women. They are vulnerable when they take shelter under the wings of their mother hen, but at least they have some protection. When they become women, they become even more vulnerable and susceptible to abuse and victimization.

It is often not easy to determine who a person is from one or two brief meetings. We may not be able, even after so many years of having a relationship, to assess the designated principal characteristics of our closest friends. There is more to our being than meets the eye. Human nature is a complex phenomenon. As we think, interact, socialize, and problem-solve, we develop and become more sophisticated. We become more intricate as we grow older. As humans tell their stories, they unravel the awesome beauty and greatness embodied in their humanness. Using stories to share our experiences is like peeling an onion. Stories reveal who we are. As we go deeper we see the more tender and amazing parts of ourselves.

We are a mystery the day we are born and remain a mystery until we die. We are not any more a mystery at fifty than we are at conception or when we were one minute old. It is not that our mysterious nature increases. It is our level of cognitive sophistication that rises. But an increase in our cognitive complexity and level of social and cultural sophistication does not necessarily increase in the mystery within us. It could be said that the worldlier and cognitively sophisticated we become, the more likely we are to lose our sense of mystery. Our mystery nature is part of being human—of being a man or woman. Our human mystery that is in the image and likeness of *Egvibhair* is *otherworldly* compared to *this-worldly*. The reason why infants and babies are simpler and less sophisticated is because the mystery of who they are is more intact and purer. Their innocence and simplicity preserve the beauty of their mystery. The simpler, and closer to the Great Being we are in keeping the commandment of love, the greater our being exudes mystery. This is even truer of many African women you meet in the remotest villages of Africa.

Many African women walk with much dignity and elegance. We are not in a hurry. The reason for this is not just that our culture requires that of us. It is not because our attire constrains us, as some think. It is in our being. Many African women carry many burdens. Moving fast becomes difficult and sometimes impossible. The majority of us retain so much in our hearts and ponder it. We are trained to remain silent about our sorrows. African culture obliges women to not talk about the injustice in their lives. We are educated to hold our silence as sacred as the acceptance of the injustices and abuses meted on us.

Many women bear the burden of their children—seven children mean seven burdens. An African woman bears the burden of caring for her husband as well, even as unfaithfulness and abuse have become his way of life. She bears the responsibility of being the custodian of her culture and traditions even though her civil and customary leadership roles are not recognized. She bears the responsibility of caring for the leaders of her church, mosque, or shrine even though their structures and institutionalization bar women from leadership positions. Taken together, these burdens impede her development and oppress her.

When African women migrate to the United States and Europe (which are more sophisticated and complex cultures), the experience can be a dizzying one. Everything and everyone move so fast. Many of them complain that everything is too fast. Many of them begin to lose their English because they cannot keep up with the pace of conversation. One of my African sisters teased, "I am surprised people do not bump into one another or get a ticket for walking too fast."

Being slow does not mean African women are stupid. They come from a place where things and people are simple and "green." In their culture, processing is more appreciated than producing. They are not used to pressing buttons and having things move. They may not be used to seeing a lot of cars in their villages and navigating their way through them, but her being is much more than her past and present experiences. Her experiences may contribute to shaping her womanhood but her womanhood remains the core of her essence and being.

Her Time: Sexual violation and emotional abuse rob a woman of her "precious time." You hear many abused persons say, "I wish I were never born. How did I get into this mess?" An African woman abused by a man would say, "He has wasted my time and my life. I wish the day I met him never existed." These statements and many others suggest that no amount of positive time gained in the future can recoup the time for abuses of her past. By relocating, she can begin to live! This relocating can be done in the form of storytelling. If she can summon up courage to tell her story, she has a greater chance to live better. But remember, she will never forget! Her experiences significantly influence who she becomes. She cannot easily brush them off or pretend to bury them. But she can begin to live a better life when she moves away from the victimizer. Within her new environment, she can begin to allow her better past to marry her future hopes so that her present can give birth to new energy and the strength needed to move on.

If she is courageous, she will tell her story to others. But it must be her choice to share her story. She can share *her story* if trust is developed. What you do and how you relate to her will speak to her being about who you are. Then she might begin to guess about your intentions. Remember that her vulnerability is likely to be the same reason why she is naïve and trusts easily. When all is said and done, her trust comes and builds naturally. Don't worry—it will come. You don't need to force it. The African woman will trust you if she senses you are not trying to use her. She will trust you if she perceives you are not merely taking her picture. She will trust you if she trusts that you are not there to expose her weaknesses. Exposing her will rob her of her only power left—her personal space. If you push them, African women can "comb" their stories for you, just so you will leave them alone. Missionaries and foreigners make this mistake over and over.

When an African woman shares her story, she is not asking you to fight for her. She is not looking for problem solving. She is not asking for pity. She is already powerful if she begins to share her genuine experiences. She is simply inviting you into her world. She may tell one experience over and over. An experience shared three or seven times in a day should be carefully listened to with new ears each time. When an African woman tells you her story over and over, she is inviting you into the depths of her being where the story has made an indelible mark. It may be a reminiscence of "the good old days." You would do well to relive that sacred time with her. If they share bad experiences with you consider yourself honored and privileged. Your listening is an invitation to become a caregiver to the storier . She is offering you a job and your acceptance empowers her.

Time connects us to space. Once we lose a sense of time, we get lost as we try to remember. Only a return to the familiar can help us reconnect when time is completely erased from memory. In other words, connecting to our space helps us keep track of time. Even the perpetrators of violence and abuse in the African land seem to understand the significance of and the relationship between time and space. When African children are kidnapped, the kidnappers lock them up somewhere in Africa and often hide them for months, even years. They isolate them from the support of family relationships, familiar space, and normal developmental activities. These kids suffer an incredible loss. Even when they escape they often have no way to reconnect themselves to their families, and it is likely they will have difficulties creating a positive personal identity. If you suspect a child is in trouble, do not hesitate to follow him or her. You will soon discover whether your instincts were right or wrong.

Her Space: A woman's image and self-esteem can become distorted when violated sexually or emotionally. When she looks in the mirror of others' eyes, what she sees in the reflection is dirt, ugliness, and failure, someone worthless and hopeless. The guilt and shame cannot be explained adequately in one chapter. These feelings of worthlessness and hopelessness do not go away by someone simply saying to her, "Forget it and move on." Sermonizing does not do it either. In many cases, even counseling or therapy is not adequate for an African woman because all contemporary counseling or therapy is based on Western theory. Yes! African women's special counseling needs do not fit into the theoretical framework developed for the Western world. Some may wonder, "What specifically makes an African woman's healing needs different from any other victimized woman?" My response may be as complex as the African woman's problems. The extreme urge for secrecy, the perpetrating structures and systems of her society, the gravity of abuses, the prevalence and frequency, the length of time it has taken for her to share, and so on. Some of these exogenous problems need to be held somewhat under control before counseling or therapy can work for a person. These helping services work because there are rules and regulations, norms, and structural and cultural expectations within the society. These systems and structures are lacking in many African societies.

The pain of an African woman's victimization does not simply go away with urging her to put herself together and pull herself up by her bootstraps. I am not saying it is permanent damage. It is a serious distortion of her image and womanhood. Her healing lies within her. Because it is a spiritual activity, she alone can choose who to help her. If you get the invitation, it means you can help. It takes art, prayer, patience, and love to be part of an African woman's healing process. Remember that anytime she sees or hears about her victimizer, her wound is reopened. If she is to move on, she must move away from her victimizer. Serious questions here are: Where will she go? Do we all have to run to America, Europe, or major cities of the world before we can receive justice? Can no one speak for the African women? Is it not possible for African women to reform the very culture and systems that have been, for many generations, oppressive and unfair to them? These questions are not meant to be answered. They are intended to help us as we journey with the African women in this book.

There are forms of relocation, namely social, religious, physical, and emotional. Relocating helps a woman begin to do some mental and spiritual cleansing, and image rebuilding. This mental and spiritual cleaning is possible in the new environment because it is on unfamiliar ground. The new environment becomes a holy ground for her. Her cognitive template begins to remap when she relocates. By relocating, she can begin to regain space and her authority *within*. Her perspective changes in the new environment, and she can begin to tell her story. Healing comes with these changes and gains of strength. Do not forget that anytime she meets the "familiar" or valid reminder of the past she recalls the scar that remains.

Situating the Story: Rape can be physical, emotional, or mental. Any one of these rapes does as much damage as the others. I have experienced more emotional and mental than physical rapes in my life. I believe these injustices and abuses came my way because I am an African woman. I had no one to tell them. When I shared with my mother, she encouraged me to "never call these experiences rape." I know she was trying to protect her womanhood as well as mine.

There are two kinds of rape. First is the *impersonal private* rape. This kind of abuse can be sexual, verbal, physical, emotional, or mental. This kind of abuse is within institutionalized relationships such as couples, families, and communities. It is not supposed to be this way. In these institutions, the relationship is approved or certified by society, the church, or the school. So it becomes even more difficult for the African woman to speak out when she is abused or raped within one of these institutionalized relationships. This is the kind of abuse that takes place in the bedroom, in the family, in schools, and in religious and social settings. Because of its subtlety, this kind of rape can be found even in developed nations. I believe women's and feminist movements were founded to address these problems.

It becomes abuse when all expectations for love are thwarted and love turns into lust and violence. It can be in the form of brainwashing, indoctrination, abuse and and subtle disempowerment. It can be very emotional and sometimes to the point that no one word or phrase can adequately describe it. This form of abuse is the most prevalent. Many women have shared how they survived this kind of violence and abuse. This kind of victimization can be very subtle and more discrete than the second. Fewer women are more conscious of it than others. Many do not directly articulate it—but you hear it in their stories. It is sad to hear them describe the darkness within.

The second kind of rape is what I term the *personal public*. Against a woman's wishes, in the full view of Father Heaven and Mother Earth, she is forced to accept sexual intercourse or undergo other forms of physical abuse that may result in bodily injuries. The more she resists the more violent and brutal it becomes. This kind of rape is very common in many traditional African societies. Personal public rape is less obvious but more prevalent in the cities than in the villages. Friends have asked me to provide them with statistics. I have promised I will provide this data-related information in the publication of my research, *African Women and Psychology of Oppression* . In the meantime, I challenge you to visit remote and hidden places of Africa and do the counting yourself.

In the higher institutions of learning, it is fast becoming a norm. Some male teachers in higher education settings extort money from students if these students are to receive grades they deserve. These male teachers demand sexual relationships from the female if the female students are poor and do not have money. In order to pay these abusive male teachers the money demanded, some of the female college students have entered the profession of prostitution. One said to me, "Sister NG, I don't want to do it. But the evil profession is necessary if I am to finish my education. My parents are very poor. The only way out is if someone steps up to give me money. My tuition and 'hand-grease' fees to teachers come from the money I make from this trade." She is poor but determined to get the education necessary for upward mobility on the social ladder. Because she does not want to give in to the sexual demands from her male teacher extortionists, she decides to go into prostitution to get money to pay the teacher. It is a lose-lose situation.

She even has to "rob Peter to pay Paul." She misses classes to go into the city to meet her male clients. The teacher still gives her very good grades when she gives him money even though she has not learned what she needs to learn about the subject matter. In the end, she is a loser. What she bought is a paper certificate, not an education. With this certificate comes less confidence and more guilt. Before she went to school, she was underpowered. At graduation, you might say, she has become disempowered. One way or the other, she is a victim.

When I was in the college of education, one of the professors asked me to see him in his office. He started with flattery : "You know you are a very brilliant student. I see your records, and you have been making As." Then he threatened, "But you know you must comply if you want to pass this class well."

In my gross naiveté, I asked him what I should do. His response, "When we go to the hotel room I will let you know," not only made me mad but shocked me. My heart started to pound as my thoughts raced. He started to flatter me as I stood there bewildered by the words coming out from the mouth of this married elder. All my respect for him dropped as I stood there transfixed. Everything he said passed over me because I was thinking about what to say to him. When I recovered from my shock I managed to respond to him that my mother told me not to go to bed with any man until I was ready for marriage. He responded with an abusive, "I can tell your mother is illiterate and must be a bush woman." I wanted to cry, but the woman in me challenged me not to.

I dropped my voice—he must have thought I was ready to give in. I asked, "Sir, are you married?" He responded affirmatively and added, "Don't worry about it." I asked him if he had a daughter and if his mother was still alive. He responded yes to all.

I felt it was my turn. I asked him with as gentle a voice as the woman in me could carry, "Are your mother, your wife, your sisters, and daughters bush women?" I saw rage brewing as I watched his Adam's apple rolling back and forth under his chin. I could tell he was struggling to hide his anger. That was my first time witnessing a black man blush from rage. I quickly managed to add, "Your women should be sorry to have a man like you."

I rushed out of his office and banged his door to the breaking point. Of course he made sure I paid for it in the most expensive way he could find: he gave me outright F in his class. I went to the Student Union president and then-chaplain, Archbishop AJV Obinna. Obinna took the case to the disciplinary committee. I was made to retake the exam, and still the professor gave me a C. I did not fight further.

This is an example of a corrupt system and faulty structures. That one C pulled my GPA in Education from Distinction to the second level. My mother commended my boldness. From that day, I promised to stand by and speak out for my fellow women. I know it is a costly mission, but I have become unstoppable.

Let's take the issue of the rape of Beauty and Belle. When I asked people why they think African women do not tell others when they are abused or raped, their responses fell into several categories: (a) they may be afraid and ashamed; (b) they think no one will believe them; (c) they don't trust the authorities; (d) the entire system is corrupt; and (e) there are no medical facilities or authorities to test and document evidence. All these responses are reasonable and authentic explanations for failure to report abuse, but they are only the tip of the iceberg. I think the deeper reason is that an African woman's (in fact, any woman's) sexual dignity is sacred and powerfully tied to her identity and self-image. She becomes a lost persona when raped either emotionally, intellectually, or physically. So it becomes difficult if not impossible for an African woman to share something about the loss of her special dignity. This is the same reason why many rape victims (African or not) do not come forward to charge their offender.

Remember the three things a woman communicates to you about herself when she shares *her story*. She wants to describe her world—her being and her time, as she invites you into her space. When she loses her being and her time due to rape or violence of any sort, she becomes at a loss in her world. In that single act of violating her fundamental human rights, her being and time are robbed. The only thing left in her world is her space. She conceals it. She tells no one and doesn't want anyone occupying that "space" in which the evil was done to her. She constantly prays, "I hope no one saw this. I hope my eyes alone and my being alone experienced this horror." She guards "that space" jealously and carefully. Not sharing her rape story is the way she protects her space, the only self-property she believes she can keep, and so she shares her story with no one.

When all is said and done, telling the story remains the single most effective form of healing for traumatized and abused persons. If they can tell it, they can heal. Yet most of the African women and children victims of abuse do not easily enter into conversations even with therapists or counselors about their dark personal and deeply felt experiences that are present in their neighborhood, in Africa, and in the global village. In some cases they do not even see or acknowledge the injustice. I want to believe that some of them have been indoctrinated to think that it is normal. "After all," they would say, "that's the way it has been from the time of our ancestors."

CHAPTER THREE
Will It Take a "Witch" to Save Child "Witches" of Africa?

Our Gifts-Our Woes: Women are very gifted. That's right, all women (and men) are gifted! With our gifts come obligations and responsibilities. *"She to whom much is given, much is expected."*

Humans are generally gifted in one way or the other. The question is, how developed are these gifts? As an adolescent, I felt so gifted that at times I would become confused and unfocused. A priest friend of mine always challenges me with a tease: "NG, focus." If only he knew how versatile my giftedness is. I am like many women. Because of how society shapes us, African women become versatile and multitasking. One woman can be a homemaker, a lover, a thinker, a problem-solver, a teacher, a wife, a mother, a caregiver, a professional, the breadwinner, an entrepreneur—the list goes on. It is a learned survival mechanism. But it often hampers us. Sometimes, we look stupid and confused. When we multitask, we often appear to be incompetent. Of course, *a Jacqueline of all trades is mistress of none.*

Every gift has its corresponding weakness. Depending on how we develop, where we are, who we deal with, and how we are received, our weaknesses may be all that those around us see. People can choose to pay attention to the opposite of our gifts and capitalize on these. All children of the earth are beautiful, good, and strong. Of course, there are few naughty ones. But we see what we choose to see in others. The more people reinforce our weaknesses—no matter how indirectly this may be— the more these weaknesses manifest themselves in us. For instance, if a child is told she or he is possessed by a demon, before long such belief is internalized and the child will begin to exhibit demonic attitudes and characteristics. The same is true of our strengths. If we affirm and validate the strengths in our children, it will not be long before they begin to incorporate these positive qualities in their personalities (even if they were not present in the beginning). I am what my father and mother affirmed in me. Looking back and reflecting on my growing up, I can attest that some of these gifts were never present at the time they were being validated.

The Mystery in Us: Have you stopped and wondered why extraordinary and mysterious events and movies engage our senses more than ordinary ones do? I want to think it is because we are mysterious ourselves. We are ordinary beings with extraordinary potentials. The mystery within us is attracted to the mystery outside of us. Humans are mysterious. Christ's coming into the world as human and God made humanness more mysterious. Let me digress a little bit. "Being all things to all people," says our brother, St. Paul, was the Creator's salvific mission for human beings. Our Christian faith holds that it took the Creator to become a creature in Christ Jesus in order to save humankind. Jesus is like us in every way except sin. He is fully God and fully human. That could be where human confusion starts. This does not fit into any human theoretical model or philosophical framework. Jesus is the fullness of mystery. As God, Christ is unlimited with what he is and can do. But as Christ's followers, we are limited in what we are and can do. As a human, Jesus went through the most horrible evil in history. Being God, his passion and death have become an epitomic symbol of many of the worst experiences in human history because he was absolutely innocent of wrongdoing but most unjustly treated. I am not a theologian, so I digress.

As humans we are limited in time and space. We are limited in what our biophysical, cognitive, and affective self can understand, explain, experience, and do. However, we are not limited in what our spirit can experience and do. In a way, our environment is also unlimited. But what we know and perceive about it is limited. The limitation of our spirit is that we cannot absolutely and permanently connect to our spirit while living in our body. Even though we are both body and spirit, we are trapped within our limitations as long as we live in this secular world. We cannot absolutely connect our spirit with our earthly self. The hinge here is that as humans we find it difficult sometimes to honestly accept these limitations. I think the problem of being human is that we are both limited and proud at the same time.

Many humans refuse to acknowledge their limitations. Because of our limitations and our pride concurrently dwelling in us, humans fall over and over. The Adam and Eve in us is indescribable. Our limitation makes us fall, and our pride makes us want to cover the fall. Excuses have become second nature to humankind. We believe we must find a way to close the gap. We are at a loss when we cannot explain a situation. We can't excuse others of what we perceive to be wrongdoing. It is like losing control, and the more we advance in science, the more humans feel they *must* find a way to explain or understand life, events, time, and space. This should not be an obsession. We don't have to find explanations for everything. There are many things that are likely to remain a mystery, and we must not frustrate ourselves trying to understand or explicate them. When something extraordinary happens we often become frenzied and fearful. We become unbalanced and our actions betray us as we try to justify why we must know the answer. I am not suggesting that we should not be responsible and accountable for worthwhile inquiries such as those done by the media, academia, and other forms for investigation. What I am saying is that we must let mysteries be mysteries, even as we try to understand them. We should not make ourselves sick from stress and depression by trying to understand that which is beyond our general human and individual capacities.

Unquenchable Thirst: Clocks, letters, numbers, strokes, and maps are some of the devices created by humans to control, explain, or understand the world and the creation of the universe. We should not let these devices control us. They are to facilitate the smooth running of societies and the global village. They are supposed to help us understand our environment and the people that dwell with us in it. In no way should they be the reason for our troubles. The human mind created these devices in order to help us solve our problems, not create more problems. If they do not help give us peace, happiness, joy, and wellbeing, then their purpose is defeated. ("The Sabbath is made for man, not man for the Sabbath.")

Living in America, I constantly struggle with time management. But I try to watch out when I see myself constantly trying to catch time. If I don't I could easily become sick. I encourage you to watch out when you start to say, "I have to finish this," "I have to do this and that," "I must go here or there," etc. My psychologist friend Albert Ellis calls it *mustabation*. Remember that bad or unhealthy habits are easier to learn than to unlearn. But our reasoning can do so much more than we can imagine if it has been schooled properly. Because some of us believe we can multitask and are multitalented, we often find ourselves racing against the clock. Prioritizing has helped me in my efforts to organize and balance my life. Very few things are truly important in this world. Only two (love and life) come to mind. Being conscious of what enhances love and life has helped me tremendously. It has helped me to become more humane and less materialistic. It has even helped me become more realistic in saving. Being mindful of what matters most has motivated me to start recycling earnestly. I believe it is in the nature of humans to give and receive love. To love is to share, and sharing is hardwired in us. When we do not share, we become stuffed and bloated.

I have learned to recycle virtually everything I use and have, including my time and talent. This is why I have started writing. This is also the major reason I am returning to the classroom. I desire to share and explore knowledge and understanding with my students, as well as receive intellectual gifts from them. Every thought, word, and action has consequences for us, others, and the environment. These effects may be direct or indirect, immediate or remote. Our motives direct our thoughts, words, and actions, and humans are incredibly motivated. Sometimes, I tend to think that motivation is a biogenetic component of humans. What we learn is how to choose from the abundance of motivational variables presenting themselves, and how to regulate these choices. While lower animals follow their instincts, humans have motives. The more conscious and goal-directed our thoughts, words, and actions become, the better motivated persons are developed. I am not referring to impulsive or compulsive actions. Our motives need to be checked and examined. Finally, the more intrinsically and authentically motivated we are, the more (I want to believe) we can help others tap into their own internal motivation. We cannot give what we do not have.

The more we share, the more empowered we become. In what follows, I present some maybe simple examples of how I share. Sharing is very simple and anybody can do it. My apartment is cleaned at the beginning of every year and I give away a lot that I do not need. I have reached a point where I believe that anything I have not used in the past six months does not belong to me. If I keep it, then I am hoarding. But I still hoard books and literary works—*mea maxima culpa*.

You always hear people say that we do not know how much we have acquired or accumulated until we move. Why wait until we move? Living simply is living happily. And living happily is dying peacefully. As I said, I go through my wardrobe every six months and give away what I have not been able to recycle. When I take a shower, I let the water run only when I need it. I do not turn on lights automatically. I turn them on when I need them and off when I don't. The challenge in all these simple practices is being able to remember. It helps me remember when I think of those who have less or nothing at all.

If we truly think of others affected by our thoughts, words, and actions, caring will come naturally. If we do this often enough it will become the *"habit"* we wear. Love is our nature. I believe it is possible to make it our habit. Love not lived becomes a fossil. We have to learn how to live a life of love if we lose it growing up. We can lose it when our self-centeredness begins to develop during our childhood and adolescence. But we can learn it again as an adult if we choose.

Another simple example of how I practice saving is in the kitchen. If I am cooking (I love to cook), I turn down the heat once the pot reaches the boiling point. After all, it cannot heat any further than that once it climaxes. The result? I have saved energy. Some of these savings I am aware of; others I am not. Ultimately, these habits are fostered by my desire to share and to love. It is an unquenchable thirst. Sharing has become a way of life for me. I feel happier, healthier, and more energized. I suppose there are other benefits of sharing which I have not yet been able to articulate.

The Innate Lies: Some argue that some level of obsession is good for humans. When not obsessive, some may argue, the drive to understand and explain is one of the highest aspirations of the human spirit. I believe it is one of the principal characteristics that distinguish us from animals and plant life. What is problematic is the human obsession to control, explain or understand that does not know its limit. This obsession does not stop with the material world. It also seeks to explain and understand the immaterial world including the *otherworld* and the spiritual realm. Again there is a problem: the lack of an objective umpire or judge. Everyone claims to be right and purports to hold the truth, especially in those spheres or regions of the world that lack adequate scientific, regulatory measures and enforcement of law and order. In these regions that include some of my African societies, where there is no framework for studying and evaluating human behaviors, some resort to spirit or religion—that which is beyond human scientific proof. Do you see how the obsession to explain and control can lead to frustration?

I have been told a lot of horrible stories by friends in my religion. Many injustices are hidden under the cover of *what the Holy Spirit wants.* For instance, when an injustice is perpetrated by a religious superior, he or she will say, "After prayerful discernment and in union with the Holy Spirit, I believe this is what is good for you." That is ridiculous. Likewise pastors who molest Africa's innocent children claim they are working under the direction of the Holy Spirit. They torture and abuse these children and try to convince the world it is for their own good. Even some of the parents have been brainwashed. You will agree with me that what those pastors do in the name of Christ is simply demonic. These pastors claim to possess maximum spiritual power over demons. Hence, they purport to have absolute control over the adherents of their religion. It is evil when humans assume absolute control over fellow humans. Only *EWURADE* is the Almighty. Some may contend that nonreligious African leaders do the same. Let me continue to sound the alarm: she or he to whom much is given, much is expected.

In the Name of His Mother: Any Christian can claim to do what Jesus would do, but very few claim to do what Mary would do. Even fewer would preach what she taught the boy Jesus. Some people claim to be Jesus, including having his miraculous healing powers. If they claim to be Jesus, they have to be Jesus fully, and not pick and choose which parts of him to be. Most of the present day false prophets do not want to identify with the Jesus who was betrayed, denied, tortured, and crucified, nor with His mother Mary who patiently and non-violently followed him till the end. Which is easier, to claim what Jesus would do or say, or what Mary would do or say? I would think the latter is easier.

I decided on the title of this chapter after I watched an ABC7 *Nightline* television program about Africa (Wednesday, May 20, 2009). In some parts of Congo, Cameroon, and Nigeria, some groups of Christian churches believe that the young members of their church are witches and wizards. These children are between the ages of four and sixteen. Their pastors convince the parents that these identified children are being possessed by demons. Hence, parents trust the pastors who promise they have powers of exorcism. The methods of exorcism are cruel and brutal to watch. Sometimes, concoctions are forced down the throat of these children. Extreme physical abuse such as beating, flogging, and even biting the children on their stomach were used. These children cried and wailed for help. Their parents stood and watched helplessly because they have been brainwashed to believe it was for the good of their children. It was too graphic and violent to watch. I had to close my eyes at some scenes. These pastors use magic and other devilish means to deceive their congregation and reptiles crawl out of these children at the completion of their exorcism.

My heart ached during the entire program. I couldn't stop crying. I wept as the program exposed the torture and extreme abuse meted out to Africa's most innocent. All was reportedly done in the name of Jesus. The heart of Jesus must have bled along with all the people of good will that day. On that day, I decided that my heart will know no peace until I see all the child "witches" rescued and saved. For the sake of even one child "witch," my eyes will know no peaceful sleep until this book is published and read by others. I can then rest knowing that I have voiced my concerns.

As I watched that *Nightline* program (Google it if you have not seen it), I imagined what might be happening all over the world. Christians cried, non-Christians lamented, and the pagans mocked the Christians. Those self-acclaimed pastors were brutal and obdurate. The question that awaits an answer is, "Which Jesus?" Surely it cannot be Jesus of Nazareth. So in order to challenge the child abusers, I choose to go in the name of Mary, mother of Jesus. Hopefully, she will remind us what her son was about when he was a flesh and blood being in the world. If those innocent, helpless children have been accused of being "witches," I like to think I am a "witch" for Christ's sake, if that is what it will take to rescue these abused children.

If the rights of children can be easily violated by the most caring people, how much more are they violated by those who do not care at all? Nothing has surpassed education as a way to empower children, or anybody for that matter. If those so-called pastors and abusers truly believe in it, why don't they use their education to progress things instead of maligning and torturing the innocent under the pretext of exorcism? In the case of spiritual exercise, who really needs exorcism? If you missed the *Nightline* program discussed here, Google

Child Witches of Africa:, Accused in the Name of Jesus. After watching the program, I believe you will agree with me that the pastors in that horrible drama are the ones who need to be exorcised. We need to do something!

Western education is known to produce positive long-term changes. But we must not wait for formal Western education before children's and women's right to life and liberty are taught to African families and societies. We need to act now! Western education takes time to set up. The mission of rescuing Africa's innocent children is an urgent one. Awareness programs and informal education on human rights should be immediate campaigns. These are sometimes more effective than formal education in most African settings where numerous injustices and human rights violations take place. It is recognized that, in some cases, academically-based rational solutions may not be effective in bringing about desired social and cultural changes.

Duty of Being Christ's Follower: On my part, I need to be reminded and connected to the Jesus to whom a woman caught in adultery ran for shelter. I need to be in touch with the Jesus who chided the disciples saying, "Allow the little children to come to me, for to these does the kingdom of God belong." I want to be sure we are speaking of the Jesus who proclaimed and cautioned, "Unless you become like little children, you will not enter the Kingdom of my Father." So what bible do the child torturers and victimizers use? Maybe they do not have one. Either these men and women child abusers have allowed their quest for money and power to block their reasoning, or they truly need to be exorcized. It could be that the demons in question are unable to reason because destitution and abject poverty have eroded their cognitive and affective abilities.

Yes! Economic destitution or the quest for excessive money and power can make many people do bizarre things and act aggressively. At both ends of the spectrum (extreme poverty or supra-richness), humans can become brutal, unreasonable, and animalistic. The destitute and supra-rich have some things in common. It is a thin line that differentiates them in relation to what they will do for money. Both groups need to carefully monitor excesses before they occur. What helps us here is our endowed love plus the authority *within*, not human might. With respect to power, the destitute have little or none left. The supra-rich may have too much.

Getting an education, developing self-consciousness, discerning our vocation, creating handiwork, valuing responsibility, serving humanity as a volunteer, engaging in entrepreneurship, and many other key human existentials differentiate humans from the lower animals. On the other hand, excess pursuit of wealth, power, and pleasure can reduce humans to mere machines or lower animals. We are the product of what we think, feel, say, do, and believe. When we can no longer communicate the language of love to fellow creatures, we become less human. My grandmother always cautions me, "Be careful not just of what you eat and drink, but also be careful of what you think, say, do, or feel." These behavioral characteristics and the choices we make form and shape us. Who says grandmas are not the embodiment of wisdom? One may say we have little control over our feelings. Yes! We do. But being able to have greater control over our feelings can be learned. We train our mind to control our feelings. It is like building a dam as a floodgate of our emotions. Once the dam has been built, we can always put a check on outflow of our emotions. We can also learn to process and respond to our feelings.

CHAPTER FOUR
The Cry of the Heart

Our Power, Energy and Force: I can imagine the Blessed Mother of Jesus crying out, "They commit all these atrocities and claim they are doing them 'In the name of Jesus.' Are they speaking of my son, Jesus, or someone else? Surely, they cannot claim it is the same boy I nursed and raised to manhood until he went out to do what he was sent to do. He lived, worked, and preached among humans. He suffered, died, and was buried. On the third day, he rose from the dead—and continued to remind the disciples what he had taught with words and deeds." Mary the mother of Jesus of Nazareth is typically portrayed as meek and humble. She is the ideal nonviolent activist. She stood by her son until the end. In her gentleness lies her greatness. In Mary's typology lies the ideal womanhood. Only the lowly, those who identify with her, can hear her humble cry. This is what makes me believe that the Lord hears the cry of those children. We cannot be silent!

As I suggested in my previous reflections, there are two characteristics of intellectual power, emotional energy, and spiritual force (power = P; energy = E; force= F): negative or positive. Every human being as well as our environment has the potential to exude negative or positive PEF characteristics. Divine grace, virtues, principles, self-control, thoughtfulness, selflessness, kindness, and most importantly, love are some forms of positive PEF.

When we exude positive or negative characteristics, others around us are influenced accordingly. What we give to others has the potential to enhance or destroy us, others, and the world around us. Others get what we have or give.

At a very early stage of development, human beings can curtail excess negative PEF. For Africans and many traditional societies, when negative energy becomes unbearable it is often termed demonic. The one exuding the negative energy is labeled evil. According to the preceding standards, the so-called "child witches" of Africa are not evil. They have no negativity in them. They are meek and humble. They are gentle and innocent. They are mostly simple-hearted and genuine. They are not witches. Their hearts are tender and their minds are innocent. They do not exude negativity. Most children simply do what they are told to do. Humans are directed by two forces, the forces from within and the forces from without. For the most part, the forces from within the hearts of children are positive. Sometimes these forces may show up in the form of mischief and fun, but they are not evil. I am certain that the cries of these children have reached the throne of Light. I believe that visitation from the throne of Justice will come to the false prophets, pastors, and all abusers of Africa's innocent young. Justice will reign!

There are so many cries for help in the continent of Africa. But there is also hope! Some of these cries have begun to disturb the world village. The citizens of the world have begun to respond to some of these cries. Rape and domestic abuse still abound. But thanks to Allah people are beginning to pay attention. The citizens of the global village are no longer unperturbed. Women and children are the targets and the most vulnerable victims. People ask, "Why can't they speak? Why can't they tell their stories?" If we have not been there, we will not understand.

Let us look at another form of violence and abuse that seems to defy eradication: cultural oppression. I call it cogno-traditional abuse. I use "cogno-traditional" to describe some of those long standing African cultural practices and traditional structures that victimize some groups and favor others. These have formed part of the victims' psychological being that very often it requires extraordinary efforts and specialized training to help them begin to believe that it should not be that way. Some social justice issues that border on well-established cultural practices are subtle but pervasive on the African continent. Many of these issues are psychological in nature. They weigh heavily on the shoulders and in the hearts of many abused women and children. At creation, humans are commanded to maintain and enhance the created world. Of course, RUHANGA did not allow us to have absolute control over nature and its evolution. The Supreme Being commanded us to love, to share our fruits with others, and to not selfishly compete with others. Hence, it is an abuse of the rights and liberty of others when we presume we have absolute power or control over them.

When African women give an inch, some may take a foot. With time it grows into a mile and eventually become infinite. When we allow a situation to get out of hand and do not put a stop to it at onset, it can get to a point it cannot be reversed. "A stitch in time saves nine" comes to mind. My point is that some of these cultural injustices are fast becoming norms. These injustices are impeding us from making progress. They have impeded African women to a near-crippling stage. What is scary is that we may not be able to move forward in order to bring about significant progress.

Celebration of Memory: Humans tend to have a very short memory. We are highly selective when it comes to what we remember. We soon forget where we were once the situation changes. We often lose interest in what was not positive and life giving. These characteristics may be a survival mechanism. We could become self-destructive if we focused on negative events from the past without attending to the positive possibilities of our present and future. No one wants to live in a past that was ugly and negative. Some remember the past as positive and live in retrospect, particularly if it was better than the present. The selective remembering that is unfair is to pretend we did not notice injustices. It is unjust to repress thoughts about the plight of the poor and abused persons. It is unfair to humanity when we refuse to remember we were once there or that we could have been where others are. It could be argued that they have taken our place on the lower rungs of the ladder that we might have a better life. When people drop down the ladder of social status many withdraw their attention and support for them. When the chasm between them and us becomes wide we lose our socio-cultural connection with them. In sum, we simply neglect them! We no longer want to deal with them.

If we display a selfish attitude, our selective remembering becomes even more negatively skewed. Sometimes, selfish attitudes tend to be associated with selective memory for our good. They help to remember those things that were pleasant and persons that were there at our beck and call. We choose to remember those we used and those who were very kind and compassionate to us. Our human nature wants to remember those persons who gave us the icing on the cake. But maturity, other orientation and good judgment help us to remember those who gave us bitter herbs that helped heal our vices and woes.

When I don't have a word to accurately describe the cry of the heart, I try putting it into art. I try singing it into a song or dancing it into steps. Sometimes, words are insufficient to express my innermost thoughts and feelings. Paintings, writings, drawings, songs, and dances are used as better representations of what I am thinking and feeling. They help me to better understand myself and those around me. Notice that I am speaking of my mind and emotions. I do not presume my spirit is not part of it. These behaviors launch me into that depth where the spirit dwells. From there I find praying and praising helpful and healing. I strongly believe we must create a space for the spirit that is in us already.

I presume that many educated opinions understand that *"Differences are not deficiencies"* Differences allow us to create our individualized identity. African women are different. These differences also exist among African women themselves. Their differences make them special. An African woman's suffering and the burdens she bears have made her special. She may be illiterate but is certainly well educated in her culture and traditions. Her life may be hidden within a mask of conformity and obedience, but I believe her spirit lives and thrives in her world. The cry of her heart comes from the life-giving spirit within her. It is the spirit of truth and beauty. It is this spirit that has brought her to where she is today. The African women's cry of the heart must be told even if no one reads them.

***Their Stories* (warning: some of these stories may be unsettling and may generate strong emotions):** The names in these stories are fictitious but the narratives are the lived experiences of African women as told by them. I tried to present them as laconically as I could without losing the gist. These stories do not mean to insinuate that African men are utterly profligate.

This is Semina from Cameroon. *I woke up this morning thinking that things would be different. But no! They are not. In fact, they are worse. It started the day I gave birth to my third daughter. He was expecting a baby boy. I did not know how to explain to him that it is not my fault. He blames me for making him feel less a man by not giving him a male child. So he has to prove his masculinity by hitting me constantly. It doesn't take much to make him mad. He harangues me and lambastes me at will. My children hide when the drama starts. If I plead, he only beats me harder. If I keep silent, he hits and kicks me to unconsciousness. One day he beat me until I fainted. And when I awoke, I noticed blood foaming from my mouth and my body was torpid. My two daughters were helplessly sitting beside me as I was lying on the floor. I don't know when this agony will end.*

This is Kwamboka from Kenya. *I am a middle child and the only girl. My image of womanhood has not stopped tormenting me and my ego. I regret being a woman. But I did not choose my sex. Why should I be punished for being a woman? I feel like I am being punished because I was born human. When I look in the mirror all I see is an ugly, weak, good-for-nothing woman. I wish I was born a man or not at all. I was denied a Western education. All my brothers are literate. "What would be the point?" my father said to himself. "She is going to be somebody's wife, anyway." My father said that any money spent on me would be a total waste. I was eager to get married, and not so much because I wanted that commitment now, but because my identity and ego have been tied to marriage.*

45

So I needed it badly. I was given off to marriage at the age of fourteen, exactly one year after my mother announced to my father that I am now a woman (I had my period).

This is Ama from Ghana. *The village gong sounded, and we knew the priest of the shrine was going to visit our village. All the young virgin girls began to tremble. I became so sick my sweat dropped like blood. From the dim light of the native lamp I saw my sister shivering. The sound approached our hut and stopped. My elder sister's name was called by this strange voice from the darkness of the night. My sister was only twelve years old. She shouted, "Nooo" as though to repudiate the evil prophecy; as if that would change anything. She had been chosen by the gods for atonement and expiation for a taboo believed to be the reason for deaths in my clan. My sister clung tightly to our mother who tried to console her with the words, "Go, my daughter. Consider yourself blessed that the gods have decided to choose you for atonement. You will remain my hero forever." My father forcefully tore my sister away from my mom. My sister held onto my father pleading for mercy and help. The cry broke my heart. As soon as part of my sister's body showed at the door, a masked hand snatched my sister away, and that was the last I saw of my beloved sister. I have lived with this pain in my heart for thirty years. It doesn't seem to go away. I don't want it to until I see my sister safe at home.*

This is Teresia from Congo. *I am literate. I received a good Western education. I was raised in a culture that victimizes. French is my second language, but I also learned English and I am just as fluent in it. I smile and sing all the time. I dance in my mind and it shows in my movements when I walk. My friends tell me that even the way I walk suggests grace and beauty. They tell me that my accent is like music. No one knows the burden I bear. It is so heavy I need to shake it off through dance. I sing away my sorrows so that I do not suffocate from thinking of them. No one understands. Unless you have been there, you cannot know. Even if I tell you my story, you may not understand because you have not been there.*

This is Amina from Ethiopia. *Something in me told me I was born great. But if I am a woman, what is this greatness? These feelings are latent and deep-rooted. But I can't talk about them—not even with my mom. She would think I was being a rebel and letting her down. I did not want to disappoint my mom. I am a Muslim. I am very beautiful, strong, and bold. But all my life, I have lived like I was a "chicken" even though I believe I am an eagle. You don't understand how it feels until you see yourself reared in a cage meant for a gazelle when you are an elephant. It hurts to be a woman.*

This is Konmma from Zambia. *I will start by saying that I think being a woman can be very onerous. My sister was beaten to death by her drunkard husband's people. They said she killed her husband.* (From the story, I suspect he died of liver disease.) *She was made to drink some poisonous concoction. They told her if she was innocent she would live but if not, she would die. Who knows what they put in that drink? I knew it was poison. My sister drank it and started coughing. My mother and I took her home from the elders' meeting. My sister barely survived. Two months later, my sister was found dead in her husband's home. Her body was covered with severe bruises and a swollen face, indubitable evidence of physical abuse. She died, leaving her two innocent kids orphans. I decided to run away to the city. I did not want to marry. I hate my people. I cannot imagine how such horrible things could be happening and no one is saying anything.*

This is Camelita from Rwanda. *I had the privilege of being my father's princess until the genocide began. I can't remember exactly how it all started. My parents died trying to save me. My one brother died in the battle and one feigned death. My sister was raped until she died in a pool of her own blood. I was raped five times by five men within thirty minutes while hiding. Those thirty minutes seemed like eternity. When I got up, I crawled out of my hiding place, whispering my sister's name. They must have taken her, I thought. Seconds later, I found out she was dead. My heart was broken. I cried silently until I choked. My brother got up from his feigned death and tried to close my mouth. I thought they said we are cockroaches and therefore had no blood. But they raped us. I never heard that humans could rape cockroaches.*

This is Kokomma from Nigeria. *I used to be very religious. I am my husband's first wife, and we were married in the church. My husband had two other wives besides me. He married them because I could not give him a male child soon enough. My boy was born after my second rival. My pastor told me he would like to travel with me to Europe. He obtained an international passport for me. He processed my visa and all the travel documents needed. I told him to keep all the documents because I did not want my husband to see them and suspect something. I was ready to do anything as long as that would get me out of the country. It was time to leave the country. Who says there is no God? My last child became very ill. My husband did not understand why I was so bent on making this trip when my last child was dying. Being a very smart, educated woman, I tried to be sly, using all the equivocations and logic I could think of in order to convince him. He even promised to reimburse me for all expenses if I would cancel my trip for the sake of our child. I told him I would need to travel to Lagos in order to cancel the trip. My phone rang and my husband must have suspected. He may have looked at the incoming call coded "my love." He let me go—but followed up using his best friend as a proxy. I was spotted with Rev. Father "my love," holding hands and checking in at Muritala Mohammed Airport. He was my love and made me feel I was the only woman in his life. I was wrapped in the love of Fr. "my love" when someone stopped in my face. It was my husband's friend.*

He made sure he locked eyes with me and then said, "Safe journey, madam," and then turned to my pastor and said, "Thank you for putting asunder what God has joined together." Then he cursed, "Shame on you!" My husband's friend cursed the Rev. Father, but I got it. That shame lives with me till this day. I cannot go back to my country. I heard my husband has married a fourth wife. My children have become motherless even though I am still living. My guilt is indescribable. Everywhere I go, I feel like I am being pilloried.

This is Musu from Senegal. *I was fourteen years at the time. I was ready for school. I had put on my school uniform and realized it was rumpled. One of the teachers from my school lives in the same compound with us. I went into his apartment to ask for his electric iron as we very often did. On this day, he offered to help me iron my school uniform. I thanked him and was going back to our apartment to change when he called me back. He said he would provide me with a wrapper for changing. I thanked him. After my dress was ironed, he started to fondle and caress me. I was scared and could not scream. I knew people would blame me. I pleaded with him not to do me any harm. He kept saying, "I love you," but what I heard in his actions was, "I hate you." We struggled until he overpowered me, tore my pants into shreds, and had his way. From that moment, I ceased to be. I hated school and started to live in fear. I missed my menstruation and knew I was pregnant. When my family confronted him, he said he would marry me. I believe he was in his thirties or older and already married. I did not want to marry the man who raped me. So I ran away to the city. Now I have two sons because I did not want my boy to be called a bastard. Even if they taunt him, he has a brother with whom to bond. My boys neither know their fathers nor wish to meet them.*

This is Teresita from South Africa. *If you ask anybody outside our nation, they will tell you that there is no more apartheid in South Africa. Yes! There is no more apartheid. But the crude subtle antipathy existing in my country is worse than apartheid. My village was peaceful until apartheid ended. Except few political and civil rights movements here and there, we were remotely removed from the evil of the segregation that lasted for years. What we have in my country now is worse—people are kidnapped, raped, and killed without anyone inquiring as to their whereabouts. A child is reported missing and that's it. When I was fourteen, I was abducted by two men—one white and one black. The black man could speak my language. It started out as though he was interested in me. I thought I saw genuine interest. I agreed to travel with him to the city after two weeks of constant visits to my family. He looked responsible. He had clean clothes and looked very educated. He convinced me we were made to live together forever. Yes, until his accomplice showed up. The white man must have paid him some money because after fifteen minutes of whispering and gesturing, my "brother" and my fiancé vanished forever. I could not cry because I knew that would not help. The white man told me we would be traveling to Italy. He raped me all night—I lost count. He must have taken drugs because I could not imagine how a human being could be that sexually brutal. I am too ashamed of myself. I feel dirty and ugly. I don't want my mother to see me. I can't stand my family anymore. I send them money frequently. My mother wants me home but she doesn't understand.*

These stories are samples of some woes that have befallen African women. Each and every one of these cases could be as prevalent in other African countries as it is in the country of the storier. I heard these and they pierced my heart like a sword. I cry every time I remember that these stories are only a few examples of the very many victimizations and abuses inflicted on my African mothers, sisters, and daughters.

CHAPTER FIVE
A Witch and a Saint

Misunderstood: I shared parts of this book with some African friends, and they said, "NG, be careful, people will start avoiding you." Others said, "My sister, remember you are still an African woman even though you may be living in America. After you publish your book, you will return to the motherland someday". Some wondered if I was kidding. "Are you serious?" they asked. "You'd better change the topic if you want anyone to buy your book." I am glad I did not change my mind. Are we not sometimes witches and sometimes saints? Yes! Sometimes we are mean, selfish, thoughtless, careless, violent—even in our thoughts, pleasure-seeking at the expense of others, inhuman, and can behave in the most debasing manner in both subtle and obvious ways. At other times, we can be loving, caring, self-sacrificing, other-centered, peaceful, thoughtful, principled, and kind.

Ignorance is part of the human condition. Sometimes I think it is a disease. Often, everyone but the ignorant suffers the consequences of ignorant attitudes and the behaviors emanating from them. When a learned person gives in to superstition, it is like an illiterate who uses a dictionary as toilet paper. Both are operating from gross ignorance. Many of my fellow Africans are superstitious. One of the reasons I studied educational psychology at the PhD level was to discover for myself the differences between belief, mental products, and superstition as they operate in the sciences of spirituality and psychology. Because the majority of my non-Western-educated African colleagues lack the scientific and technological knowledge that predispose societies to opt for evidence based methods of study and verification of things, people and events, they resort to superstition and "African science." Hence, many Africans tend to believe most things, including that people's behaviors are dichotomized—good or bad, sinful or holy, righteous or evil, etc. There is no relativity.

My Youth: As a growing girl, I heard a voice that kept telling me I was special. The voice urged me to own that there is something unique about me. But for some reason, I could not own it. I was afraid. I did not want to be different. I did not want to associate with the extraordinary. Yet I could not run away from the mystery that I am—that we all are. Whatever the reason, I was kept back for a long time from acknowledging that I was gifted and special. Stories my mother told me about circumstances and experiences surrounding my birth were powerful enough to convince me beyond any reasonable doubt. But this inner voice was drowned by the cultural beliefs and social systems in place around me.

I was a brilliant student from the start. In school I was constantly taking first place. I earned double promotion twice. I was consistently at the top of my class. I graduated summa cum laude from the University of Nigeria. But I was still naïve and could easily be deceived. Even with all the academic achievements and apparent intellectual prowess, I did not consider myself smart enough. Looking back, I know I was struggling with my self-image and self-esteem. I did not think I was good enough because I thought I was nobody. After all, I was "only a girl." Going to all-girls boarding school was a first step toward liberation. At the all-girls school there was no male-female competition. That was not quite the competitive environment I needed—though it was a start.

I thank my parents who helped lay the foundation of my Catholic faith and my abundant love for Jesus and Mary. My parents are strong Catholics. Although my parents received no Western education they were enlightened and savvy in cultural intelligence. I give thanks first to CHINEKE, and I also thank my parents for their hard work. My parents started out very poor. They recall many times when there was no food in the house when I was a baby. My mother tells the story of how her heart ached when I cried from hunger.

At the invitation of his brother, my dad moved to Onitsha with my mom and me. It did not take long before things changed for the better. They became affluent in two years. My father owned his own company, an auto parts shop. My mother became a wholesale distributor of dry fish. At the break of the Nigerian-Biafran civil war, there were two of us—my brother, Arinze, and me. My parents were rich until the Nigerian civil war (1966–1970) broke out. They lost everything during the war, but they still had my brother and me. Three years after war ended, we moved back to Owerri, the city where I was born. We did not become poor again but my parents didn't quite make it back to the financial level they achieved before the war. By the end of 1982, I had six siblings. We all attended Catholic schools. For secondary education, we all went to boarding school except my siblings who did not want to miss Mom's cooking. The Biafran war prepared me to be a great nurturer. For instance, I was the fulltime babysitter for all my siblings except the last two, Amaka and Tochi, who were born at the time I was already in boarding school. I was still their part-time babysitter during vacations and breaks whenever I came home.

I left home for secondary boarding school at age ten. While there I exhibited symptoms of a psychological illness twice—I think it was a form of anxiety neurosis or ADHD. No one knew what it was. You can imagine how that was interpreted. Everyone in school believed I was an "ogbanje" (an Igbo name for reincarnated children born to die and, if they do not die, must be witches). Some thought I was a witch and actually called me that, despite my religiousness and being a strong member of a prayer society called The Block Rosary.

Something was convincing me that I was not a witch. As a matter of fact, I thought I was a saint. I believed I was another Saint Theresa of Nigeria—Ha! Ha! Ha! Some students started to gossip that my achievements in sports and academics were coming from mammy-water (the queen of the waters). In sports, I was leading my dormitory's junior athletic relay race, 100/200 meters races, and high jump. At first, no amount of name calling or verbal abuse by students could change my understanding and belief of who I was. I had many secret admirers but only one close friend—Stella Achike. She was the only one brave enough to come close. I need my friends but I also wanted so much to continue achieving. I was tortured within, dancing between two worlds. I was carrying a heavy responsibility trying to be who I was without losing my friends.

The Young Shall Grow: From class four (tenth grade), I began to pay attention to the name-calling and labeling. I could not afford to lose any more of my very many loyal friends and admirers. I saw myself starting to live in one of the two worlds at any given time. Sometimes, I had my friends because I would feign achieved failure. Some other times, I would excel in my academics and did not care if I had friends or not. At some point, I was tired of living in two worlds one at a time or even simultaneously. I wanted to belong, but I needed desperately to excel and continue achieving. I needed to relate and so the peer pressure won out. I started to play dumb. I wanted to be "normal." I stopped sharing my dreams, my internal stirrings, and unique experiences. I started to achieve failure. My academic performance began to drop. Going to boarding school was the first time I lived outside my parental supervision. Parental supervision changed hands from Mom and Dad to teachers and school-mothers.

On the eve of the day I was to leave home for Abbot Girls' Secondary Boarding School, my father had a nightmare. He dreamed that he was carrying me on a motorcycle from Owerri to Ihiala. When he came to a bridge, I jumped from his motorcycle and into the river. There in his presence I turned into a snake and swam away. He stood there and cried to no avail. My father recounted that he woke up in pain and sorrow. My father was so worried that he discussed the possibility of not taking me to a boarding school with my mother. My father's fears heightened when he remembered I was only ten. I was my father's princess, and he would rather choose death than allow anything to happen to me. He calls me "Nne"—mother. My father was so protective that even though he would have loved to see me get married he became overjoyed when I announced I would like to become a Sister. All these attachments weighed so heavily on my father that he could not see me leave home. Hence, the horrible dream.

My mother convinced him with the following words: "Are you just finding out about the mystery surrounding this child? From the moment of her conception, there has been one mystery after another unfolding like flowers. She is the child of our first love and our virginity. I want to believe she is given to us by CHUKWU. We have named her Ngozichukwu—God's Blessing.

"Remember the psycho who used to hang around the Assumpta Cathedral, who came to the maternity ward when she was born?" my mother reminded my father. "That man said she should be called Chinyeremngozi— CHI has given me blessings."

Coincidentally, that was the name my grandmother chose for me afterward. "If the Creator wants to stay there and does not prevent the devil from taking her from us, it is not our battle but CHUKWU's," my mother concluded. "Let's get her ready," she urged my father. "I still need to buy a few things to complete her prospectus" (the boarding school list of things to bring). With these words, my mother tried to calm my father. My mother's wisdom and courage prevented me from missing my first opportunity to attend a higher school of my choice.

For a year or more in Abbot Girls' Secondary School, I was the youngest girl in the entire school, which had an enrollment of more than a thousand. For some reason, I was not intimidated at the initial stage. My academic achievements, athletic talent, and the love of my parents gave me strong leverage. It did not take long before I started to flourish in this new environment. I changed from a shy, withdrawn child to an outgoing, outspoken Ngozi. When my parents took me back to school for the second term, they made a point to see the school principal, late Rev. Mother Eucharia Anyaegbunam. My mother asked Mother Eucharia, "Mother, what do they eat here?" Then she continued, "She came to this school shy and timid; now she is gbazakwin [excessively outgoing]. She came to your school not talking, and now she talks and doesn't stop. I used to scold her and tell her to speak up. I don't know whether to say 'thank you' or 'now we are in trouble.'" All of them laughed, including me. I fell into the sitting-chair in Mother's office, laughing. For me those statements were so funny. My mother turned and said, "Look at her. Just look at her." She simply shook her head.

It was at Abbott that I had my first dream of flying. Prior to this, anytime I was dreaming and was in danger or needed to escape from harm, I would look around for a body of water to dive into. Once in the water, no impending harm or danger could match the swiftness with which I could swim. Yet, in real life, I did not even know how to wade in water. I had not been in the water again in my dreams until the one last time in 1999. I will discuss this more in *The Mystery of a Calling.*

Every race and culture has geniuses and gifted children. The systems in place and the socio-cultural beliefs and practices provide platforms for their development or lack thereof. Traditional African cultures, customs, and practices do not have elaborate and robust platforms, resources, or systems for very gifted children. If the child is physically strong, chances are the child will become a strong farmer and/or warrior. Male children have more opportunity to use their physical talents in traditional African societies than female children. On the other hand, women are not expected to show masculinity. In some traditional African societies, the young languish and rust as their innate gifts and talents are not actualized. If their gifts are spiritual, affective, or cognitive, they have no outlet for them. They remain latent until nature causes them to erupt like a volcano. That is why gifted children tend to do strange things. They have very unusual experiences whether awake or asleep. Gifted children are a bundle of mysteries. They have extraordinary gifts but can become either withdrawn or excessively outgoing.

Gifted children could easily become mischievous, particularly if they have physical strengths to match their latent gifts and they are not channeled properly. They are looking for appropriate outlet for these talents. Remember that their world is deep but at their stage in life, they lack adequate symbolic skills to communicate it. In some cases, they may not have developed adequate symbolic language or vocabularies to articulate what goes on in their mind and spirit. Adults do not understand them either. These extrapolations stem from my personal experiences. Gifted children sometimes leave adults filled with awe and wonder. Because traditional gifted African children perceive they could get in trouble if they talk about their dreams and experiences, they button up.

In Africa, when people cannot make sense of children's mysterious experiences, they label them either an *ogbanje* (as among the Igbo) or a reincarnated ancestor. For the most part, girls are more likely to be labeled ogbanje.

I've come a long way—a very long way. There's no going back. To go back would be risky; it would be worse and even more dreadful. So I have chosen to move on. In 2000, at the peak of my crisis related to whether I should stay with this particular religious community (I chose to make it anonymous) or not, I asked for a thirty-day retreat. I needed to be alone with the Supreme Being. I needed to consult with the Master Jesus about my calling. Ever since I discovered my inner power and energy in that thirty-day retreat, I have never looked back no matter what the trouble or problem. And I don't think I will now. By the same token it is my urgent desire to help as many of the world's women and children who are victimized and abused, particularly those in Africa. I pray to be a voice for them—to as many as would be sent my way. I earnestly want to be a source of encouragement to African women and children. I may stumble at times: three steps forward and two back. But it's been a forward march since 2000. I will continue to march on until all African women and children are free. We are not free as long as there is one African woman or child chained by oppressive and longstanding cultural practices. We cannot relax until all human beings enjoy the authority endowed by our MAWU. Some African women have not articulated the many faces of injustice present in their lives. Occasionally, it is hard to work with such women. But we should not relent.

Many people stand out as strong helpers in our struggles. Others are inhibitors. My image is a runner in a race. When those we support fall down, we must stop to help them get up. We must not jump over them or avoid them. Love and grace make it possible for us to stop and help. It takes more effort to jump over or avoid the obstacles in our way than it takes to stop and help. Over the years, I have learned to overcome obstacles that pose themselves as stumbling blocks. When we learn to love all obstacles become building blocks that help us build a strong fort. If I feel the obstacles are becoming overwhelming and are beginning to pull me out of the race, I move closer to the center of the track away from people. It helps me to regain my focus and singleness of heart. I do this in the form of prayer, reflection and retreat. These spiritual exercises help to sharpen my focus again over and over. Prayer is an indispensable part of my life. Just as food and drink keep us alive physically, prayer keeps me alive spiritually. I can do nothing without help from the Almighty One. If I fall, for whatever reason, I bounce back through the sacrament of reconciliation.

Made for Greatness: I have learned not to be too scared of the future. I embrace difficulties, hardship, or suffering when they are present because experience has taught that through them I have become the person I am today. Problems are not our enemies—they are friends and colleagues. They toughen us and sharpen our mind. "Problems are cowards; they present themselves when they want to be solved," says Osuofia (a Nigerian comedian and actor) in one of his movies. The more problems we solve in life, the better we are at it.

At times, the future may scare me, but experience has taught me that there is nothing I can do about neither my future nor my past. I have learned to trust the love and continued guidance of the AlphaOmega. I have learned to rely on the strength within and the powerful maternal protection of the *Samokpu* (Immaculate Virgin). Eternal graces have helped me heal from my past timidity. I have been healed from the weaknesses which society and the church have placed on my womanhood. By divine grace, I have grown from the wisdom obtained as a result. I believe I am wiser than I would otherwise be.

As I repeatedly say, I love to learn. I love to ask questions. Like many of my friends, I enjoy learning new things and understanding them better. Like many spiritual people, I am comfortable with the virtues of humility and amiableness. But I am also proud and strong. I believe that we are all made for greatness (no matter the shape, type, or size of it). I believe this greatness for you and every woman. ZAMBE empowered us "to till and develop the earth" (me, others, my environment, *all*). When we cultivate life in this world, we ennoble our humanness and testify to divine nature. We are all *humus*—earth, relating to heaven. Together we are Mother Earth and Father Heaven. I am a woman. More than that, I am humus in my being, created in the most beautiful and mysterious image and likeness of our Maker. I feel I must contribute my share—and I am passionate about it.

I have a friend. Before we met, we became great friends via her authorship. Her name is Immaculee Ilibagiza, and she is the author of the *New York Times* best selling *Left To Tell: Discovering God Amidst the Rwandan Genocide*. You probably know who I am talking about. Since we met, she has become my adopted daughter. I now fondly could call her Imma. Being an African woman and having visited Rwanda, I connect so powerfully to her story. If you have not read that book, grab a copy. You will not be the same after reading it. I invited her to the inaugural conference of African Women in America (AfWiAm), where she became the keynote speaker. Immaculee is an intelligent woman. Her authority, powered by her love, is observed just by holding her book in your hand or coming into her presence. She recounts that her generous spirit was learned from her parents, especially her mother. Like most women, Imma is never demystified by suffering or abuse. She is a goddess. A very few know the stock of which such African women are made.

Sisters caught in a whisper by a hidden camera at an AfWiAm conference. *left*: Immaculee Ilibagiza author of *Left to Tell*, keynote speaker 2008 AfWiAm conference,

It is popular to think that women have more emotional endurance than men. That is to say, they embody patience, mystic powers, and love, which allow them to weather terrible experiences. Experiences that men would not tolerate at all or for long form the strong women we have in our society today after they have gone through them. This is what leads me to imagine that the Creator is much more than the anthropomorphized image we have of the Great Being.

I do feel sorry for those who fight about the name and gender usage for BAMBA. Many African languages do not have that problem since our pronouns are unisex. For instance, among the Igbo people, there is no differential usages such as "he," "she," "him," "her," "his," "hers," or "its." One word is used to denote these pronouns. You will know whether it is a man, woman, animal, boy, or girl in the context. Nonetheless, permit me to join the Christian's debate for a moment. First I would like to join the camp of Jesus Christ of Nazareth who called God Father and taught us to pray the "Our Father." If CHINEKE is the Mighty One in battle, the Almighty, the Defender of the innocent, these qualities are ascribed to the male physical prowess. I would also like to join the camp of Julian Norwich or the author of Isaiah who chose to ascribe feminine attributes to the Great One. If the Supreme Being is such a patient, tender, loving, and enduring mother, these are not male characteristics.

Julian of Norwich says these qualities are of women. For all I know and through human stories and experience, it has been demonstrated that our Maker is both our Father and Mother. Therefore, it is a human problem, not divine. It is humans who are either male or female, becoming man or woman. Yes! Jesus became human. Assuming human nature, Jesus has to be one of the two—male or female. His Mother, the Blessed Virgin Mary was the woman who gave birth to him. She could not have been a man if she was to conceive and bear a child. So the sex of Jesus's humanity should not confuse us about his divinity. MUNGU is EGVIBHAIR. ALLAH is mystery. Let us stop anthropomorphizing the Great One. When we humans lack the language to address spiritual matters or mysteries, let us be humble enough to close our mouth and gaze with awe and wonder.

By the way, this book is not about what pronoun we humans ascribe to our Creator. If anything, it is to recapture that authority which is ours from the time we are conceived in our mother's womb. Our Creator has blessed all humankind with this authority whether one believes in the OTHER existence or not. Whether a witch or a saint, we all need our Maker to actualize the authority given to us.

The Struggle Continues: Being where I am today was not achieved on a bed of roses. But like the pangs of birth, my bad memories have been well replaced by my dreams and visions.

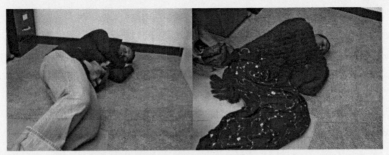

Sisters taking turns to sleep in AfWiAm office floor in order to get the work done: Agnes Ntow, Board member AfWiAm, Miss Ghana 2010 and contestant Miss Africa Beauty Pageant 2010 and Ngozi Udoye, president of African Women in America

I struggled to find the right community. Four times I was asked to leave the convent; five times I asked my Lord Jesus and his Blessed Mother what they want from me. I was powerless but I had choices. I prayed and cried, pleading with OSEBRUWA to show me the way. Many nights I soaked my pillow with tears. I fasted and prayed, begging the Mysterious One to accept the humble sacrifice of my sinful self. I prayed that love would continue to draw me into a friendship with humanity and the Creator. I prayed that Jesus would behold me every moment and smile to his CHIFWE and say, "Thank you, my Father, for creating her. Thank you for the Spirit that dwells in her."

Forsaking the religious life or leaving the Catholic church is not an option for me. I am convinced I have a vocation to consecrated celibacy. I am also convinced I have a message for the church. However, I was not sure if God was calling me to live in a convent with a lot of other women, some of whom I perceived to be very weird in character. Every effort was made to quench my vocation—first time, second time, third time, and even a fourth time. Sometimes, when I tell my story, people think I am making it up because it is so bad it does not sound real. I was thrown out for being too fragile when I was in my teens, for being too brilliant and over-achieving, for being too attached to my family, for being too mysterious, for being too outspoken and bold, for showing too much love to people outside of the community, for being too zealous, or a combination of these. All these *toos* and the superlatives are their exact words. One of them even threw me out because, "Ngozi, you are *too* perfect. This place is made for sinners and not for saints like you." Whether she was serious or sarcastic, I found this one particularly funny. She got me canonized without my permission while I was still living in this sinful world! That shocked me the most because I thought we enter the convent for our salvation and that of the world. I found it not just funny but very strange and disturbing as well. She probably thought that all she saw in me was not me. If she had discovered her own authority, she would have easily identified the same in me.

The last group kicked me out because I wanted to study. I had a full scholarship, so that was not the issue. I was asked to leave for being too ambitious. I was being led to where I am today. Now I am in a religious family where I feel and believe I belong. My religious brothers and sisters can never be outdone in nobility, prayerfulness, humility, and love. Together, we strive to live after the heart of Jesus, whose love is indescribable. Love did not stop Jesus from becoming human in order to save the whole creation. If we love, all other things fall into place. We pray every day for the grace to live in humility like Mary the Mother of Jesus who, though she was carrying God, did not make herself distinct from the other Jewish women of her time. We want to be the ambassadors of Christ's love to all we meet. That fits perfectly with my personal goal in life. I want to be Ngozi (a blessing) to all I meet. Finally, I have found where I belong. I can struggle like any other human being, not afraid of being misunderstood.

Called by Love: My vocation is a mystery. Like I mentioned earlier, you will see the details in my book, *The Mystery of a Calling.* I can also say that your vocation is a mystery. We can't weed out the Divine will. It is so lush and vibrant that it outlives all humans. This world was created by *someone*. The ONE is the creator, sustainer, sanctifier, and the home of all that exists. I wasn't at peace whenever I decided I should get married or wanted to forget about this religious life business. There were many nights of pain, anger, frustration, and near mental breakdown. But the spirit was strong. At one point I was plagued with anxiety neurosis. That was a fancy name the doctor gave to what I was suffering. I don't care what the doctor called it. All I know was that all those years, I believed "the devil sat on my shoulder and taunted me." The weight did not break me. I believe it was allowed for a nobler reason. My uncle, Msgr. Peter Onyebuchi, took over after my parents could no longer help me. After trying to shoot down my vocation they tried one last time to stop me from entering the convent. No one knew what was happening in me. But our Maker knew.

People can help—but for a limited extent and time. Human beings do not last very long in their humanitarian projects, especially if they do not see immediate yields. Generosity is eternal. Help is not. The first perdures but the second ends. Yes! It is because we are human. We are limited and finite creatures. Humans help until they are no longer needed. Helping is human but generosity is divine. Because it perdures, generosity blossoms into a beautiful virtue when humans cooperate with divine grace. Help lasts as long as the helper lasts. Through very many different people, I enjoyed the divine generosity which sustained me all those years.

The spirit speaks to me through dreams. Through dreams I was reassured, from time to time, that all would be well. Sometimes the Spirit would appear to me in a sudden trance (my onetime spiritual director, Fr. Jim Noonan, OCD, told me a term for it). Fr. Noonan was the one who challenged me to pay attention to my dreams.

He said, "Ngozi, you are so active and busy during the day that God can't even get your attention. So God waits for you to go to sleep, and then the Mysterious One who owns us speaks to your heart and mind."

WAAKA wants our undivided attention all the time. I was hearing the divine voice as well as the many talents and gifts speaking in me. That led to a confusion that lasted for several years. My family was as confused as I was, but they always supported me. Many who cared did not know how to help me. But they still stood by me, sometimes. Our Maker knew how to help me. The Great One is always by my side. BAMBA used many caring persons to nurture and support me. After many years, I have learned to stay strong once I believe something is Divine will. *Love* is my measuring stick. By the grace of our Great One who does amazing things, I do not err as long as love leads.

Sometimes, when I look back, I am amazed at how I was able to come this far. I believe it is because I am a *woman*. I was born with extra emotional stamina. I was born with a tremendous amount of patience. The cultural victimizations of womanhood under which I grew up forged the virtues of patience, love, and endurance in me.

Prayer of Thanks: Thanks to you, my Maker, for creating me a *woman*. I can't wait to see you, never to be separated from you again—the *Shekhinah* Glory. In your beautiful image and likeness I am created, and I am adorned with the choicest, most precious gifts of love, tenderness, strength, endurance, meekness, energy, intelligence, beauty, and faith. Finally, you gave me the gift of hope with which I trust you will always be there for me and with me. I am truly the daughter of a Goddess. And I believe I am a goddess. I am meek and strong, I am obedient and powerful, I am poor and wealthy, I am ignorant and intelligent, and I am simple and sophisticated. I am human and I am mystery. I am a sinner and I am a saint. The beauty and emotional energy of my womanhood are rays which radiate from the core of your being in me. They dazzle others and illuminate the glory of *YOU*

CHAPTER SIX
Power Versus Authority

A Woman's Secret Tool: I may not have power, but I have authority. My authority is unshakable. I want to draw a line between these two. As far as I am concerned, the two are not equipollent. We easily confuse them. Power and authority are remarkably different. Power is felt by those outside it, but authority is known by those possessing it and acknowledged by those affected by it. Power can be described and measured, but authority is immeasurable. Authority may be revealed through power when there is a legitimate presence of power. Every authority contains in it power, energy, and force. A person's authority may be evaluated using these as a yardstick. Not everyone has power, but everybody has authority. It is our birthright from our Creator. Only the Almighty Being has absolute authority—infinite power, energy, and force. Like I said, I may not have power, but I have much authority. One day I was chatting with one of the bishops in whose diocese I had worked. He was teasing me, saying that I am not afraid to talk to him. He actually "accused" me of being bold because I am not afraid to talk to the highly placed officers and heads. I responded to him with a question. "If I can hold a conversation with the Almighty, why should I be afraid of talking to you, who are mere servants?" I would be afraid of talking to someone whose position in relation to the divine is questionable or doubted. But as far as I know, every person I meet is a child or servant of the Most High unless proven otherwise. This does not preclude the necessity of paying due respect to legitimate authorities.

When we say African women and children are powerless, we are correct. But it is not contradictory to say they have unquestioned authority. Humans are endowed with the authority of *within*. This authority is indestructible. Many African cultures contain a good number of doors that close off equality and justice for women and children. Power is still unidirectional, favoring for the most part adults, particularly men. Any society that upholds inequality and injustice inflicted on a group or class of its members stands to lose. I will say more about this shortly. A society that denies equal opportunity to women hurts itself. Albeit, while men take up power positions in Africa, the authority of women remains indisputable. The giftedness and PEF (power, energy, force) that are part of women and children's authority are still intact. In many cases, the PEF qualities become underutilized, unutilized, or moribund. The women and children's *within* authority will not equipotentially be engaged by African societies. The continent suffers the consequences of this injustice—any injustice. To a greater or lesser degree, everyone suffers the consequences when some people are marginalized.

Kinds of Authority: There are two kinds of authority, namely the *without* authority and the *within* authority. The without authority has two sources. There is the constituted without authority, and there is the self-obtained without authority. The constituted without authority is that which is invested on the holder by the majority of a group's population. *Without* authority can also be self-obtained, meaning that the holder rises up to it by achievement, popular admiration, or by virtue of a group's need for leadership. When self-obtained authority is taken by force, it can easily turn into dictatorship or tyranny. Constituted without authority is that which accompanies positions of office and headships of nations, systems, groups, and societies. In any given population or group, only a select few have this kind of authority. In many African communities as in some conservative world religions, women are outright denied this kind of authority. No one has been able to provide worthwhile reasons why women have been disallowed from taking up *without* authority. African women like many others are still searching for answers.

Within authority, on the other hand, is obtainable by anybody. It is the kind of authority that is inherent in our being. If within must be evaluated, love is the source and measure of it. The more love a person has and gives, the greater and higher the level of this authority. This kind of authority is more powerful and longer lasting. It is the kind of authority that tends to be more credible and trustworthy. It is the authority that is appreciated, respected, and favored by the human race. It is hidden in many cases and not as ostentatious as its counterpart. Within authority is unsullied by attack and resistant to destruction. It dies only when we die. Juxtaposed, without authority seems to be wished and admired more. But the truth is human hearts yearn for within authority as it is already hardwired in us. It is within our reach. It is attainable. Without authority is reserved for a select few. Even though we may wish it, it is not intended for everybody.

Without authority is more administrative in nature and does not lend itself to direct contact with the masses or the grassroots. It is limited with legal boundaries. For it to survive, it has to be structured and highly systematic. Without authority is not as liberating as within authority. Within authority reaches out to those different from the possessor. It does not fear differences. It actually prefers to have direct contact with the masses and those at the bottom of the pyramid of social stratum. Because the within authority is liberating and void of fears, it very often wins popular approval. People naturally and willingly volunteer to be part of this kind of authority, not because they fear the repercussions of not being part of it, but because they cherish it. We greatly admire it when we come in contact with the possessor of within authority.

At first, within authority is non-threatening to the without authority. But as time progresses, it may. Whether it feels threatened depends on the nature of the without authority holder. As the masses join the one who possesses the within authority, the without authority holder may start to lose followers and sycophants; hence, the fear and threat. But if the without authority holder possesses an equal amount of within authority, there is stronger mutual support. In this case, rather than fear or feeling threatened, the two (headship and subjects) complement each other in mutual support, working toward sustainable development for the common good of the society or group.

Love defined by faith is the natural characteristic of within authority. When obstacles block the way of within authority, it does not bulldoze, surmount, or avoid them. Within authority penetrates an obstacle in order to achieve the common good desired. One time I had a dream in which I penetrated a wall in order to enter the hall of the men of the underworld who had seized the bishop's keys to the cathedral. You will read more about these dreams in *The Mystery of a Calling*.

Identifying and Learning Our Authority: Although it is an inborn trait in humans, the within authority needs to be nurtured and cared for. It is developed through learning. Paradoxically and mysteriously, it is learned under the hammer blows of experience. Jesus learned obedience through suffering. To be schooled in the within authority can be demanding and very often frustrating. No wonder many humans who possess the within authority do not emerge as having it. In the process of developing our within authority, it is very easy to give up. The temptation to slide back is huge. Perseverance is an indispensable virtue here. Our societies, their cultures, traditions, and experiences draw on our cognitive template—our *equator.* (Equator is the word I used to denote the cognitive self of the EPCAS field developed in my other writings. This will be explained a little bit in Chapter Nine) Sometimes they help. Other times these drawings make it harder to develop our within authority. But once learned and fully developed, within authority is as lasting as eternity, as constant as the northern star, and as sure as the morning. Though it is fragile and easily vulnerable, the within authority does not break nor does it die easily. The within authority is the source of power for most women. It is this kind of authority that has powered me to where I am today.

Political and economic lives in many African countries can be very capricious. Many aspects of the culture and politics lend themselves to high instability. Democracy seems to be practiced on whims. This capriciousness creates other problems that can range from subtle corruptions to obvious corruptions and high degrees of unaccountability. African citizens have been intimidated by their government to such an extent that they are afraid to challenge or question policies and decisions. Their coping mechanisms are as strange, weird and unique as these problems. The few literate manipulate the many illiterate. The populace tends to exhibit a blithe attitude as if they are unperturbed about the systems and structures in place. But the truth is that human endurance has its limit to unjust tolerating sufferance. I don't want to believe this cannot be changed. A certain level of systemic dependability is required to make learning of authority feasible. It is passed on from one generation to the next. Within authority is learned the way cultures are learned. One does not need to attend a formal school setting to learn cultural sets needed to survive in that society. People learn within authority in the cultural contexts of their everyday life of thinking and problem solving.

CHAPTER SEVEN
The Power of Authority

The Unspoken Language: Try as we may, there are some constructs that are statistically immeasurable. Some of these are love, truth, beauty, and grace, to mention but a few, yet we know them when they are present. Every creature knows love when it is present. An infant in an adult's lap knows and experiences it when there is love or lack of it. That the infant lacks the language capacity to respond does not negate the fact that she or he knows the presence or absence of love. There is no language as universal as the language of love. Whether one understands another's spoken language or not, love is known, felt, experienced, internalized, and understood when it is present.

When one cannot communicate in a common language available in one's environment, it does not mean that the one lacks the basic intelligence required to adapt in that environment. The dignity of our personhood is beyond the ability to speak a given language or not. It lies in our love-capacity. Our abilities can shine in any environment once that environment avails us opportunities. When I decided to do my Masters and doctoral programs, everyone thought I could not do it except my illiterate mother and my advisor, Professor Ron Morgan. Being an educator par excellence, he saw my hidden learning abilities and scholarly stoutness. His love and belief in me powered me to great heights. To the extent we can give and receive love, to that extent we are motivated humans. As a matter of fact, the dignity of our humanness is not measured by our rhetoric—it is measured by the degree of our *within* authority. I want to believe that the nobility of my personhood is measured by how much love I give and receive from others with whom I share the earth. Love transcends human language and culture.

Authority Denied and Love Violated: African women and children have been treated in the most dehumanizing ways more so than any other class in the global village. Some of their experiences are awfully incredible. They don't need to become raucous before the world hears their cries. Sometimes, I wonder whether it is because we cannot speak out. Or is it that the world has lost the universal language? Could it be that women's language capacities have been maimed by long-standing cultural evils meted on us—so we don't know how to speak? Whatever is the cause, the effect of love-lost is making the weight of power-grip unbearable. At this time and in this dispensation, there is no more time for altercation and unnecessary rancor. We can make deliberate choices for liberation. If African women must choose liberation and freedom, we have to engage in activities that unite us. Yes! United we can—divided we fall.

The rate of injustice and abuse is becoming astronomical. Men's proclivity toward abuse of women is fast becoming the norm. The most frightening aspect is that the government and community leaders seem unperturbed. These evils are fast becoming the order of the day. Everyone lives in fear. Love has become elusive. Neither the law nor community love is present to protect the women and children. Everyone apparently pays no attention. You cannot imagine the number of women and children who have had to face the torture and agony of cultural injustices and social ills on a daily basis. (Please visit www.afwiam.org for issues facing the African women and children.) Some people have baptized some of these issues "culture" and have confirmed them traditions. They are evils. They are abominations and taboos.

Our ancestors allowed some things out of ignorance. They did not pretend. But we now know better. We know that many traditional practices that disfavor and marginalize some groups are wrong. The era of ego-culture-centeredness is over. We cannot continue to say, "It is our way of life; our forefathers did it." In this twenty-first century and with all we know now, there should be no room for excuses. If we women are still the custodians of the African way of life, we must strongly refuse to accept some of these practices that marginalize African women and children. Any culture that is not life-giving or problem-solving should be defenestrated.

I may not know how to shout and scream against all these injustices, but I sure can cry. I want to join the tears of so many women who have been denied the joy of sexual pleasure because their genitals have been irrevocably mutilated. I want to cry with the young girl whose culture supports boys-only education. My heart wants to lament with those women who have become numb to the beating and physical abuse of their husbands and brothers. I wish to mourn with my fellow women whose tears have watered their husband's grave because their widowhood has turned into a curse. I want to cry with those women whose only knowledge of sex is through rape. I wish to empathize with those women leaders among us who are told that their place is in the kitchen.

Let us take it up from here. Look at their faces. Listen to their heartbeats. Watch their body language. Use your heart, not just your eyes. You can hear their cries. Imagine you are one of them. It is not hard to imagine. But it will be impossible if the imaginer lacks love and the within authority. If the imaginer lacks love, she or he may not believe or even understand these pains and sorrows. If you can't help, do not add to the problem. For sure, one thing we can all do is respect them. Let us start by respecting these women and children. Have you ever considered that some of the many pictures taken of African women and children could be done without their permission? Some of those pictures seem to expose only the ugly side of the continent. How about taking pictures without showing their faces sometimes? That is respect. That is love. That is lawful. It is not only when we suspect we could be liable to legal justice that we become lawful or loving.

Her Paradoxes: Although this book is about my struggles, it could actually have been about any African woman or child. So many times I changed the title. This is not because I am undecided about what to write. The book was nearly finished before a befitting title was decided. I am aware this is unconventional. I was just pouring out on paper my daily struggles as much as I remember them. I tend to be loquacious when it comes to sharing my experiences. I also included the experiences of the African women and children I work with. When I asked my friends and colleagues about writing a book on *The African Woman*, I did not receive a positive response. As I listened to their feedback, I concluded they believed I was taking too big a bite. This forced me to change the title as often as I received feedback in order to accommodate their suggestions. One note I must make about all these interactions between my friends and me is that while many of them are academic colleagues, some are not women. and when they are, they are not all Africans. Some said, "The title is too idealistic and ambiguous." I should have given them the manuscript, and they would have seen how confused I was at the time I sought their advice. Nonetheless, my friends could be right. But the disclaimer I make here is that this book is about me. It is about womanhood; it is about African women and children. It is about me and it is about you. But all about me, about womanhood, and African women and children is not this book, meaning that one book cannot claim to capture all that African womanhood is. It cannot claim to provide a synopsis of what African women or children face. With this I am free to dare. So let's continue to explore.

If I had maintained a stand, given the injustices I suffered in the hands of my culture, and my understanding of what I knew about the African woman and her child, this book would have been in your hands sooner than now. I don't think we know or understand fully well the stock with which African women are made, nor can we fully grasp the many abuses and degradations they face. We may not be able to bring assuagement of any kind to the victimized African women, but our understanding may change the way we perceive the next African woman we meet. Honestly, I want to know myself and eagerly want to understand the African woman. Our understanding enables us to appreciate, respect, and walk another's path, maybe in her or his shoes.

This is a question I ask about the African woman: "Did their experiences mold them into who they are, or is there something in their genes?" I do not want to make any claims yet. What I wish to request is, come along with me and let's make this adventure together. We may never know or understand fully why many African women are subjected to such unjust treatment and yet they maintain sweetness and beauty. But we may begin to peep into the crack to see if we can begin to ask the right questions about the African woman even if there are no answers yet. The one thing I can say at this early stage is that the strength of an African woman is discovered in her weaknesses. Her power is revealed in the suffering and hardships she undergoes. And her authority is known through the abuses and violations she endures.

An African woman is full of paradoxes. She is simple but sophisticated, weak but strong, voiceless but eloquent, powerless but full of authority, and she is said to be evil but full of goodness. If I had appreciated these puzzles and mysteries, I should have finished this work long before now, even without a title. Maybe, I would have been the first in her-story to write a book without a title. I can hear you say, "Here she goes." NG must be NG. I spent many years trying to solve the puzzle rather than making efforts to understand and appreciate the womanhood—even that which is in me. I do not want to claim that I have understood womanhood even though I am a woman. I don't have to.

Part of this book is an effort to understand the strength and authority that power an African woman and her child in the face of all the atrocities and evils that surround her and into which her culture has plunged her. The African woman is a mystery. One of the sisters eager to introduce me to another sister said, "Watch out for this one, you can't really figure her out." I quickly concurred, "Sure, I am not one plus one that will always equal two. I am made in the image and likeness of the Creator who is all-mystery. I am therefore mystery moving about. Don't even try to figure me out because I will be very difficult to be put on a mathematical or laboratory table." This is one of the reasons I came to the conclusion that the reason humans created numbers and figures is so we can control our world. It is so that we can continue to figure others out.

The Source of Authority: As I mentioned in Chapter Three, humans have developed figures and letters in order to avoid being overwhelmed. It is humans' efforts to avoid being intimidated by this great universe that prompted the invention of all philosophy, science, and technology starting from the invention of numbers and alphabets. Imagine how this world would have been without clock, date, time or space calibrations, maps, drawings, and so on. Eternity is scary and many people dread thinking about it. So we use figures and letters to help us put things in check.

We do not need figures to know love. We also do not need to be learned in order to begin to love. Love is hardwired in humans. Experiences show that love can be thwarted and distorted. If love becomes distorted or thwarted during the early stage in the human development, many things can go wrong in our adult life. But that does not mean we cannot love again. It may mean that our love can become skewed badly. It can become selective, exclusive, irrational, and lustful. Nonetheless, we can still learn to love.

Love is the only power an authentic authority has. We are all imbued with this authority. It does not need to be explained or understood. It is the divine trademark of ownership in us. Take it or leave it, the more we want to control or manage our world with numbers and letters, the more it eludes us. Whether from natural cause or human wickedness, when we are thrown into a deluge of mayhem or pandemonium of chaos, we lose control and become hopelessly helpless. This causes great frustrations and confusions even when it is Mother Nature that has rebelled. With prayer, wisdom and authentic authority we can live in our world peacefully and happily. We may still maintain a good level of serenity and tranquility even in the midst of grave disturbing circumstances. Love is the only ingredient that makes this possible. With our within authority, we don't need to pursue happiness. We only need to tap into the Source within our being. Peace, joy, happiness, contentment, and many other virtues are some of the natural fruits of within authority. With our within authority, we will begin to believe that the Creator, who has loved us into existence, will not let us down even in the face of extreme catastrophes. Our within authority helps us to hold on tranquilly.

CHAPTER EIGHT
Mission Versus Employment

I am one of those who have come to believe that I can do it if I can dream it. I believe I can do all things in Christ who strengthens me. The fact is there is so much to do. How can we be unemployed in the midst of so many services needing our attention? A missionary is never unemployed. When one vineyard is done, another needs us. Our mission could become our business, and our business could become missionary grounds. Whether we are fired, our company has closed, or we have been forced to retire, we are never out of a job if we believe we are missionaries in this world. We may not get the job we want or the well-paid position we seek. Whether our job is menial or stipendiary, there is a relevant question to ask here: "What does our Maker and humanity ask of me *now*, in this moment?"

Toward the end of my doctoral program I started to send out applications and resumes to any job opening I spotted, perceived, or identified. Each one I sent, I would kneel beside my bed and pray over it. At the same time, Stephanie Toman and I (Travis Proffit joined later), in consultation with Dr. Elizabeth Udeh and Mary Toman, embarked on a mission of founding an umbrella organization for all African women living and working in America irrespective of class, creed, and country of origin. The African Women in America (AfWiAm) was born out of a conscious attempt to bring all African women together as one voice (with the help of their American and Caribbean friends) to enter into a dialogue with African governments and community leaders about the issues concerning African children and women. The organization was founded as a forum where African women, individuals and groups would have a platform to begin to tackle the problems facing Africa's innocent children and powerless women. I was feeding this newborn organization from my pittance. So I needed a better job. As a PhD candidate, I started to look for a faculty position in colleges and universities so that I could return to the classroom for better pay. The Great One who sends us on mission must have said, "It is not time, NG."

One day I was praying over one of my job applications and this voice spoke to my inspiration. It was as clear and precise as any message could be. The voice said, "Why are you asking me for a job when I have a mission for you?" Then I answered, "But my job will be my mission once I get it." The voice asked me again, "Whose mission, yours or Mine?" I answered more piously this time believing that this was truly a divine voice, "Your mission of course, DINWENUM." The voice said, "Well, then stop searching so hard. And stop getting frenzied about it. If it is my mission, I will send you. You don't have to search for it. I will come to you." The voice died. I woke from my stupor. I had fallen asleep from exhaustion on my knees beside my bed. I continued with my AfWiAm mission. I threw all my energy, power, and force into making sure the mission stands. From then, every person I met became my brother, sister, mother, father, or child.

Employment is Taken: On the eve of the Feast of the Assumption, I traveled to Mundelein Seminary of the St. Mary of the Lake. My religious brother, Msgr. John Essef, had invited me because I had asked to see him. I heard the voice again through Msgr. Essef, to whom I had cried concerning my need to get a well-paying job for the mission of women and children. My reason has always been to take care of the financial aspect of my mission. Notice the way I use the term "my mission." Monsignor said to me, "God is calling you to some mission great and huge. Things will not be easy for you. It is going to be painful. I can assure you that you will suffer, but you will not be abandoned," he said. "Remember what I told you in 2005, and I repeat it," he continued. "You will be the 'Oprah' of the Church. [Oprah! I murmured in me. That is fun; I don't mind. At least she is not doing badly.] All that God is asking of you now, NG, is for your *yes*." "But, Monsignor," I said in tears, "What do you mean? I need to pay my rent, I need to eat, and I need to take care of my basic needs. I need money, Monsignor." He responded with as much empathy as his voice could carry, "Money is mammon. You do not need money for the mission God is sending you. If God needs money as a tool, God will send people who have that tool. What God needs from you is *yes*. He will send you the tools you need for the mission. At any given time and situation, He will send you fellow missionaries who may have the tools you do not have. Remember, it is God's mission and not yours." Those were powerful prophecies. At last I got it. It is God's mission and not mine. At the end of that visit, he called a group of prayer warriors who had come to the conference to pray for me. There were five or six of them. They laid hands on me. It was one of those sacred moments of my life.

Exactly one month after my job application prayer, precisely on the feast of the birthday of Mary Mother of Jesus, September and a couple of days after my birthday, I was fired from the job that was my source of livelihood. That was not the first time I'd hit rock bottom in my life. My director at work had wanted to fire me on my birthday, but thanks to my friend who had planned to celebrate my birthday, I took a day off. I have been swept off my feet so many times that I have learned to fly. I fly in dreams as well as in real life—even though it is with a different kind of wings. No danger or evil catches me off guard, unless I am distracted from being in tune with the Christ in me. If we retain the vision innate in us, the built-in sensors hardwired in us by our Creator will always alert us of what is to happen. The movies will be played to us either in our dreams, intuition, gut, premonition, and/or perception. You will read more about this in *The Mystery of a Calling.*

When I was fired from my job, I was not angry that I was laid off. I was angry about the process. The manner and method of the firing was more humiliating and unprofessional than any process I could have imagined or experienced. The reasons proffered were baloney. Every case can be mooted but that does not mean that it is necessarily debatable. That was not the first time truth was twisted in order that the boss could have his or her way. I am not saying it is always their fault. Maybe my credence and naïve attitude toward issues caused this to happen over and over. I promised myself that that was the last time I would make myself vulnerable by my naiveté. I tried to keep the incident covert, but the more I tried, the more I bled within. I felt like a woman who was stripped naked and raped in the marketplace. From that experience once more I was reminded to pay attention to the African women who are violated and victimized on a daily basis. Just as we go to school to prepare and train for any profession, I felt that these incidents were schools for me. I was being prepared for the mission ahead. Like many African women, I kept it all to myself. That was the power I had—the power of my story. I shared with necessary protocols, my family, and a few friends. Immediately, they came around to shelter my nakedness until someone would provide me with clothing. With that horrible but simple experience, I feel I can now easily identify with the women and children to whom I am being sent. With many African women, I began to wonder what the future holds for us.

After I was fired, I had no choice but to look for another temporary job so as not to go into huge debt immediately or become homeless. Within a short while, I became financially desiccated. I felt bad not so much for myself as for the new AfWiAm mission founded for the African women and children. I was becoming angrier with myself and with my Creator as days rolled into months because I could not find a well-paying job. I became an absolute spendthrift. I was very angry and depressed. I lost my prayer zest and my sprightly presence. My "spiritual tank" seemed to have dried of its fuel. But I knew that I must continue to PUSH, as Fr. Ejike Mbaka describes persistence in prayer. "PUSH means Pray Until Something Happens," he says. I took my pain and anger to the sacrament of reconciliation as often as they surfaced. That is the only safe place I could tell my story. I confessed how mad I was with my director who fired me. I confessed how angry I was with my Creator more than anybody. One of the priests at the confessional prophesied that maybe losing my job was the only way God could get my undivided attention for the mission He could be calling me to. At first, I did not want to agree with the priest's prophecy.

After a few months, I was forced to accept as reality the fact that I lost my job. It became almost impossible for me to find a well-paying job. At this point, I totally resigned myself to whatever divine plan was willed for me and not what I desired. Gradually, I started to regain my strong belief, namely that the divine will is the best for us. The effervescent cheerful NG started to come back. My prayer zest returned. All worries and anxiety vanished. I became peaceful again. It was simply a miracle. No one who saw me could tell I had passed through some ordeal. My energy level and love for the mission with women and children returned with full force. My bouncing spirit reseated itself in my total being. I became whole again. I started to spend more time in prayer. I prayed for light. Even though I did not immediately agree with that one confessor, I felt empowered from confessions. The power of the sacrament of reconciliation had started to work in me. I regained my authority and my internalized balance. I was ready to go.

Mission is Given: Ordinarily, people are sent on missions. Someone has to send us before we can go. When a mission is given, we receive it. Even if we think we have taken on a mission without someone sending us, the people for whom the mission is taken are the ones sending us. Ours is to say, "Yes," and oblige. I lost my job at the time the mission of founding AfWiAm was peaking. I threw all my energy, talents, and time into the planning of our inaugural conference on October 17–18, 2008, one month away at the time. The members and board of directors worked hard to ensure the conference was a success. Meanwhile everyone was talking about the economic downturn. The recession was deepening. I felt like talking about it was giving ordinary Americans a fever worse than the recession itself. At one point I wondered whether the media was helping or killing us. The two-day conference came and was a huge success. More than two hundred ten persons participated. Seven African women dignitaries, including two African women ambassadors and a Wyeth principal officer were present. Our records showed that those who attended were natives of nineteen different African countries: Cameroon, South Africa, Zambia, Zimbabwe, Rwanda, Ethiopia, Uganda, Congo, Eritrea, Togo, Nigeria, Sierra Leone, Liberia, Ghana, Kenya, Tanzania, Burundi, Somalia, and Senegal. Also natives of United States, India, and Mexico were present. It was truly an international gathering.

Thanks to Loyola University Chicago, her compassionate and amazing president Father Michael Garanzini, SJ, and her wonderful students, staff, and faculty. Thanks also to our sponsors from within the United States and from overseas. And finally thank you to our wonderful board of directors. Everyone worked together like a family.

After the conference weeks rolled into months, and there was no hope in view for a good paying job. The economic situation got tougher and tougher. I called the voice that had spoken to me, "Where are you, Mr. or Mrs. Voice? You'd better speak up or I will consider you a fake. I do not need to go into a stupor again. Come out and let us talk face-to-face with my eyes open and my mind alert. How can I pay the rent? What about all the debts and credit cards?" The voice vanished. Maybe it was scared off by my anger. Maybe the voice knew that if it talked to me I would insult it and dismiss it. Temptations mounted. All the teaching offers I was getting were outside Illinois. I was scared I would be tempted to move on and leave the mission of AfWiAm just incorporated in the state of Illinois. I was confused again. I prayed harder and harder for divine intervention. Once again, my energy level started to drop, and I cried many nights.

I believe the Holy Spirit came to me in a dream and reassured me. I woke that morning and it was obvious that the Almighty was with me. I was strong again. That was how I continued to dance between strength and powerlessness, trust and hopelessness, faith and joblessness. It was a tough dance. When I brought my struggles to my religious community they reaffirmed that I was being called to something. Their corroboration affirmed my belief and this was very helpful. It became very clear to me, it seemed, I was not allowed to have a job that could take me away from the mission.

I had a nervous breakdown. My family sent me money from Nigeria so I could go back for vacation and my parents' golden jubilee celebration. I became strong again within the first week of my two and half months in Africa. I was in my village for two weeks. The rest was spent with the lovely women of the rural lands of West Africa. During this short time in Nigeria, I was able to raise all the money I needed to travel within these countries. The fever over the economic downturn had not reached Nigeria yet—or maybe people were still in denial.

I went to the remotest areas of Nigeria, Ghana, Gabon, and Cameroon and spent a few days in Togo. My zeal was rekindled. Throughout those weeks and months I stood once again face-to-face with the suffering of African women and children. Their distress jumpstarted me. It was as if I was being updated on the mission field. It is very easy to forget what African women and children go through when we have been in America a long time without visiting the motherland, Africa. I was touched by their stories, and they changed me forever. I felt humbled as I was exposed to firsthand experiences with all the issues that face Africa's beautiful women and innocent children. When I returned to my village after visiting the rural women, I became disgusted with the mansion that is my father's compound. The size of my spacious room made me angry. I started to sleep on the floor as a reminder of my women friends and the time I shared their mat and earthy floor. My mother probably thought I am still the strange woman she has always known me to be.

I returned to the United States from my West African mission and the economic situation was still dire. Jobs were harder to find. "I should have stayed in Africa," I said to myself. After all, so many missionaries and researchers are going to Africa and settling there. I reminded myself that if this mission is a divine call, then it must be everywhere. The Owner of Missions sends us to where the need is and not where we think we should go.

We are Sent not Hired: I love to pray the Scriptures. They speak to me in a direct and personal way. One morning I came across the parable of the vineyard owner as I read chapter 20 of the gospel of Matthew. "No one hired us," say workers in their response to "Why do you stand here idle all day". Maybe they said more than that, such as "We have our resumes and job applications. See! We are here in the job market. This is where the employers come for us."

Another day while I was at prayer I heard the voice of Jesus asking, "NG, why are you wasting your whole life doing nothing, all in the name of looking for a job?" I responded like the men in Jesus's parable but a little angrily, "No one has hired me. Can't you see that jobs are hard to find? People are losing their jobs, not finding them. Here, I have the best résumé and great qualifications." I wanted Jesus to understand. So I said more than the men in the Bible. "Anyway, I am a woman," I rationalized. I can talk as much as I want, just like I can cry whenever my heart is rendered. It is my birthright. In fact, I am surprised that the men in the Bible answered kindly to the vineyard owner who asked, "Why are you wasting the whole day doing nothing?" If it was me I would have said to the vineyard owner: "What do you mean I am standing here wasting time? Would I be standing here in the job market if I was lazy? I am hoping that someone will come out, even late in the day, to hire me for an urgent need in his house." I would have answered the vineyard owner not quite so politely as the men in the Bible—even at the risk of losing the job before I got it.

Poverty and unemployment can tend to make us unproductively inactive. When someone doesn't have a job, he or she feels helpless, and such a feeling can keep him or her down. One situation leads to another, and this breeds a worse condition and perpetuates the situation. It is very easy to be caught in the vicious circle of poverty, helplessness, inactivity, worthlessness, and further poverty. But we don't have to become inactive or feel worthless. We still have a choice and our authority. I felt like challenging Jesus when he whispered into my ears, "NG, *why are you standing around wasting your life in the name of looking for a job*?" But I managed to answer him, quoting the men in the Bible, "No one has hired me." I was immediately reminded that there are tons of things to do—service to people, communities, and humanity. It may not pay huge or even at all. It may only pay "a silver coin a day." I felt challenged by the Lord Jesus when he said, "Well then, go and work in my vineyard." I felt so fulfilled when I went back, providing services to women.

I was running the organization without a dime in our purse. At one point I felt like someone running without legs. But I have become unstoppable. I thought I could try raising the money myself with the help of African women in America. I had done this before. So I shifted gears. I sought African women in Chicago. I sought them out in their shops, on the streets, in the malls, at the stores, and wherever I met them. We developed relationships and began to share stories. For the sake of all the African women and children who are going through torturous abuse and unbelievable victimization, we committed to our *yes*. No turning back no matter how long it takes us to get there.

All energies came back. My plans to visit the women and the children of East, Central, North, and South Africa were revamped. I would like to visit them and reassure them that the African women in America have not forgotten them. I would like to visit them and encourage them to form women's groups modeled after AfWiAm—without regard to class, creed or tribe. I want to tell them that they need to come together now and not wait until there is trouble or war in their land because once there is fire on the mountain it's *run, run, run*. I would like to remind them to reclaim their within authority.

Our Missionary Journeys: Our workplace should be one of our mission fields, and we must keep this in view at all times. That is when we receive the joy and fulfillment that our paycheck cannot give us. Our personal mission statement must match our workplace's mission statement or policy. Even with very good pay we can easily become fatigued, stressed, and depressed at our jobs if we do not find a mission there. When I lose focus of my vision I feel I have to take all kinds of tranquilizers in order to keep up with the dizziness. Sleeping that used to come naturally vanishes unless I take pills. Some people indulge in painkillers, drugs, alcohol, pleasure, and other diversions.

In this country, as in much of the developed world, production outshines effort or process. But we must know that productivity or the money from it does not satisfy us or fulfill our mission in the same way as the process or the joy of doing it. Everyone contributes to the final product. We may never know or see the others involved in the process. But that does not mean they do not exist. When we make our jobs the places of God's vineyard and not just some company or place of work we go to every day, we will begin to feel a unique and authentic fulfillment. When we make our job the mission fields we will receive a joy and energy that our paycheck can never give us no matter how fat it is. The signature statement in my e-mail address reads, *"Working with and for God is the most beautiful thing that can happen to human beings."* I insert this statement so that I am always reminded. Divine mission is the purpose of our existence whether or not we believe in an afterlife.

Only human beings are created with a mission here on earth. When we see our jobs as part of our mission and begin to act accordingly, little by little, we will begin to fulfill our Creator's will for us. We don't have to leave home or country and travel to a foreign land to be a missionary. The only missionary journey we ever make in life may be our daily commute to and from work. I have become energized from the moment I embraced my work with women as my mission on earth.

During an economic recession, people became afraid of losing their jobs. I believe some become frozen with fear. We can become so preoccupied with protecting that which we love that we could easily stifle growth. We can become emotionally burdened and stressed out. Psychology informs us that our productivity output changes under significant input of negative emotions. This may be because our problem solving frame is not at its best under intense emotional state. We are not supposed to be depressed from working—we should rather be depressed when we do not work. A few of my friends tell me that during an economic hardship they find it more difficult to shed weight than other times. You would think that without so much money to spend people would eat less. I believe that losing weight originates in our mind and trickles down to the level of feeling. If I am always stressed and not peaceful, trying to lose weight might make me sick.

Some simply work to get paid rather than to make a difference in someone's life or society. I am not an economist. I have not measured economic activity but I know that the proverbial *"Onye ejebeghi nwankwo achi, na anu uda ya"* ("Even if you have never been to nwankwo achi market you may have heard of its fame") can be applied here. Some of us who are not experts in economics do not understand theories surrounding recession, yet we are caught in the flame of it. Because we do not have educated opinion, interest, or knowledge about an economic recession does not mean we are not seriously affected by it. Some suffer the consequences more than others. When I hear from colleagues and friends about what is happening at their places of work, I conclude it is a sign of the times. Some resort to disparaging and maligning their colleagues. Workers could easily expose their colleagues' mistakes in order to win favor with the boss. In the event of a job cut, those with the most red marks get fired. Trust levels at workplaces seem to have dropped. Money matters become central issues and the subject of many a discussion. African nations seem to be in constant and perpetuating economic recession. I'll let you judge for yourself what could become of Africa's political and civil lives of the people.

With the permission of economists and experts in capitalism, let me attempt to simplify the phenomenon for a layperson's understanding. I am a missionary to the world. Here, I am representing the poor and simple people at the grassroots of society. I am presenting the point of view of many ordinary people and those ranked on the low end of the socio-economic scale. I want to look at their philosophy for a few minutes. Economic recession means that there is a general slowdown in economic activities in the lives of the majority. Therefore, spending stops significantly. Okay! The question most commonly asked is, "Where did it recede to? Why did spending drop and for whom? Where did our money go?" Some may have expert ideas or answers. All I know is that someone or something did not swallow the money. It is not lettuce! It would not help to start debating where it went. Experts need to sort it out so that we do not repeat the same mistakes. An African proverb cautions us about repeated mistakes, "If an aged woman falls twice, the contents of her basket will be counted." If we continue to make same mistakes over and over, we may easily become a laughingstock.

There is something I believe everybody can do. We can all go into the "vineyard." Every workplace can be turned into a mission field. If all the workers, irrespective of arrival time or position of power, receive the same pay or closely in range, we can be sure it will take only one day for the global economy to balance itself. Again, I admit I am not an economist. Some may read this as naïveté and others as not making sense at all. The question is, "How much does an American—much less an African—care about sophisticated economic theory when he or she is hungry, homeless, uninsured, and unemployed? How much does an average American who is struggling to survive and has no future care about economic theories? Okay! If the world's population is nearing 7 billion, don't we have up to $7 quadrillion (that is if we can count it) in all the world's treasuries? If my arithmetic is still correct, we would become millionaires when the assets are distributed among the world's population. I know at this point you may be tempted to drop this book. But please, before you stop reading, let me ask a simpler question. "What is the difficult arithmetic here? Even our grandmothers who have no Western education can solve this problem. Why are experts still having difficulty in solving this simple arithmetic? Let us try the wisdom of our grandmothers. They taught us that love x hard work + competition = sharing^2 of happiness. Let us allow them to teach us how to love in the midst of a healthy competition. Their wisdom is amazing and at times unbeatable.

CHAPTER NINE

Standing on Your Feet When They Cannot Touch the Ground

Have you or someone you know ever been fired from work when least expected? Did your boss let you go when you were least ready? Has someone who held power over you decided that you were no longer part of the group and asked you to quit? Have you ever been extremely frustrated or disappointed by another's unfaithfulness? Have you ever wished you were an eagle so you could fly away to a distant land? If you answered yes to any of these, do not skip this chapter. But if the answer was "No," skip it and move on. I said earlier that I have been swept off my feet so often that I have learned to fly. I have developed wings that may be little known. The secret is that I do not allow my emotions to take over. If I do I may not be able to take off as fast and swiftly as I want. Like everything else that flies, my wings have two sides, with their compendious feathers. Because I am a left-minded, my right wing bears the most demanding aspects of flying. I take off and land with my right wing. To stay in flight until I reach the destination, no matter how long the flight, I need my left wing.

Right wing: Critical-thinking feathers. I became fledged in this model of self in 2000 to help me cope. Later I told friends it is my personal critical thinking strategy, which I term EPCAS model coined from **e**nvironmental, physio-biological, cognitive, affective, spiritual component of ourselves. I have allowed myself to become a full-fledged expert in answering these EPCAS questions. I have also developed it for other African women as a method of helping projects and awareness programs.

- My *environmental* self asks the following questions: Supposing there are only seven of us in this world, who or what would they be? Can I give as much as I receive? What have I done to improve the life of one other person today, this week, since this incident, etc? Will this community miss me when I am gone? What vacuum would be created if I should suddenly die? Could I fill it now? If all the trees, plants, animals, and my surroundings speak, what would they say about me?

- My *physio-biological* self asks the following questions: In the long run, what is good for me, versus what gives me pleasure? Can I stomach a few bitter foods for my health? Is my body controlling me more than my mind? Can this pleasure or gratification be delayed? Is the long-term effect of this immediate pleasure good or bad? Am I clean and in shape? Am I eating what is healthy, or am I eating what is unhealthy because I like it? Am I eating more or less than I usually do—if so, why? My *physio-biological* self also tells me to remember my grandmother's wisdom: This body you carry is made up of what you eat and drink, what you do, and what you think.

- My *cognitive* self asks these questions: Am I still in touch with my authority? What is the difference between me, my pet, and my computer? Can there be anything or any person I would prefer better than myself? Can any human being say they care for me more than I do for myself? What power and authority do I have over others in this situation? Who am I?

- My *affective* self asks these questions: By this time tomorrow or next year, will I still feel this horrible? Are these feelings harming or healing me? That is, are they sustainable, emotive practices? Can I still love in spite of pain and hurt? Have I lost my power to love and care? Am I peaceful—if not, why? And what can I do to change my feelings? What are the limits of my control? Am I trying to do the impossible? Why do I hurt? And so on.

- My *spirit* asks these questions: Let's say I have only one hour on earth, what is it that endures? What will I take with me? What is important—what is not? Where is the Supreme Presence in this? And where am I? Is this condition eternal? How long will this situation endure? If I die now, how do I want to be remembered? What do I leave as a legacy? With what will I greet my Creator when I return?

The answers to these questions are as personal and individual as our faces. But they are as useful as food and water.

Left wing: Internalized, balanced feathers. I developed this model for coping during the time I needed to juggle a lot of human agencies and experiences. It was during the time I needed to maintain my tranquility amidst all the negative experiences bombarding me.

- Loving others in order to live: I make conscious efforts to opt for the poor and needy. I pay critical attention to my body and my spirit. I attend to those around me. I make others comfortable while in their presence as well as when they are absent.

- Service and the joy of fulfillment: I choose to work and live as a family rather than as a

101

competitor. I work to serve, with a mindset of making a difference. I make conscious efforts not to work for money only. I constantly choose to use money to serve.

- Living for others by sharing: I struggle to live my life thinking of others' good. I strive to be less vituperative of others. I make conscious efforts to talk less about others' negatives and faults. I try to be at peace with everyone, forgiving others even before they ask. Humility is still a huge struggle. Because I am *"sophia"* I frequently ask questions. I am not afraid to ask for help.

- Flying with both wings: I rely on my right wing from time to time. What are my choices— what is really pertinent? How do I choose wisely in the midst of all that bombards us? If forgiving is becoming difficult is it because I am rationalizing and forging blamable excuses? Or, *has all reasoning gone on break?*

Notice that the right wing has only questions while the left wing has an internalized model of behaviors.

My dream has always been to help people understand how much authority God has given us. I believe that when we reach this realization we become empowered. From this point we begin to be more conscious of how we can reap the benefits of being children of God. We become enthused about helping empower others. At this point, we earnestly yearn to make a difference. When we actualize our EPCAS PEF, we can begin to make a positive difference. This is one of the reasons I came to America. I went into the convent for that reason. I went to graduate school for same purpose. I became an educational psychologist in order to be equipped for that vocation. Whatever your training is, I want to believe that our mission on earth is the same—to make a positive difference.

When the global economic difficulty made it almost impossible to raise money for AfWiAm's mission, I kept up the fight. I would go to the office, write one or two grants and prepare to-do lists for the volunteers. I felt like someone trying to run without legs. But I also felt I was struggling not to stop. I kept hoping and believing that if this mission is from the throne of the Omnipotent One, the Owner will send laborers into the Vineyard. Even when all the ends of the tunnel were dark and the future seemed bleak, there was a strong hope that came with the reminder, "It is God's mission, not yours, NG." That has kept me going.

Dignity of Human Labor: I am still running without legs. I am still dancing. The style has changed. The speed, agility, and beauty have not changed. When I decided to change the style, I chose a caregiving job again. When I care for others, I feel cared for by our Creator. I have experienced that many times in the past. On a serious economic note, I observed that caregiving jobs are fast becoming more available for many African women in America who have not had an American education. When they come from Africa in search of a better life and greener pastures they discover that most of what they heard about America back in Africa is ephemeral. A rosy picture is painted by the media. The economic façade is well presented to those in foreign lands. Many of these women are learned and well educated in their home countries. But upon arriving in the United States they find out that jobs are not as readily available as they thought when they were back in Africa. Then they enter into one of the caregiving professions—from a home caregiver, pastoral care, to a registered nurse. I chose to identify with many of my fellow African women in America.

Friends mocked, some shuddered, others pitied me, and a few wondered if I really had a PhD. They could not fathom that someone with such an honorable and highly qualifying degree from a reputable Jesuit University in Chicago could stoop so low. What is the difference? I asked. When I travel to Africa my mission to women and children is care. When I am here in America my mission is still care. In Africa I don't get paid, in America I do. I don't know why they don't get it. I refused to explain. I hear all these parodies and I chuckle. At the end of the day, I do some spiritual defenestration by which I jettison all these caricatures of me into Lake Michigan. My energy stays robust and bouncy. I want to continue serving. I did not want to drift far from my desire to serve and care. I have begun to love the work since I found out that many African women living in America are caring professionals like me.

Humans are the most ennobled of all created order. Humans are wonderfully dignified at creation. It is very easy for people to say, "There is dignity in labor." Oftentimes, I think this statement is one of human rhetoric which we recite off without an in-depth thought or critical analysis of what we say. Sometimes we forget that the dignity in question is not something ontological to labor. It is the human-dignity which we bring to whatever work we do that ennobles it. The concept of dignity is part and parcel of being creatures of a Supreme Creator. No job has dignity until humans engage in it. Thus no job should be called menial. The job we do does not bring us low. Instead who we are, the love we bring to it and how we do it raises the dignity of that labor.

Nurtured to Nurture: I kept the story to myself. I have my motive—I have always believed that the best way to gain back all we have lost is to serve. Serving roots us in our humanity and makes us humble and noble at the same time. I did not want to leave the baby organization just incorporated in the state of Illinois.

Done! Thanks to my cofounders, our board of directors and all AfWiAm members and supporters. Now that the organization is founded, rooted, and standing, I am going back to teaching and to women organizing. I believe this story must be told. I hope reading this book will motivate you to tell your own story. You never know who can be helped by listening to it. When you tell the story of your mission, your struggles and your perseverance, (even if no one reads it), you become stronger and happier. I believe I am more confident of my authority than when I started. I can no longer be set back by labeling and name calling as in the past. My education helped but I don't think education itself did it. What my education and migrating to America did was get me more exposure and security. They have set me on the road for quest for wisdom. I have become empowered because I have discovered who I am. That is why I have begun to tell my story. I believe I have been nurtured and trained by all these years of experience and by the many different people that came into my life. By reading this, your love have powered me to greater heights.

CHAPTER TEN
The Secret of Her Strength

My Belief Everything changes except the Supreme Being, who paradoxically is the source of change in the self. The knowledge and belief that only CHINEKE is permanent can be consoling. It fills the African woman with hope when she thinks to herself, *This too shall pass.* I reached my spiritual prowess when I came to the graced realization that this place is not my home. When grace reminds us of the shortness of life it releases energy and revives the motivation in us. Even when our lifespan extends to one hundred years it is still short. When we place our lifespan and eternity side by side, the comparison looks foolish. Working for eternal life unleashes tremendous power, energy, and force within us to care for others and our world.

Working for that which endures and that which will carry us into life hereafter is more energizing than working for that which ends here. Working for Father Heaven helps us to do well with Mother Earth. Working for eternity propels our hope and regenerates our capacity to love. I call this *living-in-the-eternal-presence.* I do what I do here on earth remembering that I am here a short time. It is a belief that may be difficult to articulate. We know it when we have it. We then capture it when we experience it. When you experience it you love it. You will not let it go once you experience the awesome living in the *here-and-now of the Eternal Presence.* When you

107

come in close proximity to a person with the gift of eternal presence you don't want to leave. That is why prayer is relaxing and consoling. At prayer, we are in the presence of the One who is the eternally now in the self.

All belief systems have a common element—something that endures versus the ephemeral. An African woman holds on for the sake of what lies ahead. Her children and her children's children may benefit from her endeavors even if she herself does not. This may be part of the reason for her emotional elasticity. She neither fears failure nor gloats over success. I consider failures to be stepping stones toward improvement and achievement. All failures are successes that fall outside the standard calibrations measuring instruments devised and determined by humans. When she becomes attached to measuring tools that is when an African woman is at a loss. She does not measure. For her, there is no failure because the Redeemer lives. She is constantly hoping that things will change for good. Love is the power of her protection. Every difficulty and the problems that come with them are surmountable because there is *someone* above and beyond it.

Prayer and Reflections: Prayer is a balm for my soul. At prayer, my mental environment is cleaned of the junk that clutter my space. At prayer, my soul becomes soothed and refreshed. It is also my life cleanser. In prayer energy wells up within me and my scattered being grows calm. Prayer and reflection bring me into the Divine presence. The Light shines on me during prayer. The more the Divine Light illuminates my life the more I realize my utter unworthiness. Prayer reminds me of my dependence on the Creator and my absolute need for God. My personality is more extraverted than introverted. I have what one of my friends describes as a "shouting personality." Yet I survive by my introversion. Quietude and serenity are indispensable parts of my life. When I do not pray I become restless and agitated. When

I have not had my quite time I become less productive and my focus diminishes. Prayer is the fulcrum on which all my activities and experiences revolve. Prayer directs my thinking to eternity and helps me remember that this world shall pass. Prayer connects me to the Supreme Being and sharpens my power, energy and force. Prayer has been my unchanging companion when everything else is changing.

My prayer is more relational than recital. It comes natural to me to imagine a conversation with spiritual beings. The more I pray relationally the more apt I become at it. These days it comes more naturally to me than in the past. I believe I have more dependable friends— spiritual and earthly, now than in the past. I connect with my friends as often as OCHAMACHALA grants me quietude. It can be seconds, it can be hours. My joyous and sprightly personality attracts very many beautiful friendships. I didn't use to have as many friends as I do now. When I was younger, I used to be very lonely even in the midst of many friends. Some of my friends could not connect to the depth where I liked to live. We always argued and ended up with misunderstanding. Thank heavens, that period is over. Now I have more friends than people know. I cannot do without them. I am at my best and relate better with my friends when I have had enough solitude. When we connect to who we are we become better listeners. It is not difficult for me to bask in the love of MAWU. There are other mysteries about these friendships, but those will be addressed in my work, *The Mystery of a Calling.* In my aloneness my eyes become open to things that are more important. Friendship is the greatest gift humans could be given.

Soaked in the love of the Creator, I find it life giving to love others. I do not need to be verbose about this. All I want to say is that when I pray I tap into the divine love which makes it easy for me to love. I believe that when we perform any good act, for instance, we are tapping into the eternal goodness. Same can be applied to when we love. I can love when I can tap into the Divine love. When I stop praying I become more egocentric and selfish. When my life of prayer and reflections weakens I become malnourished and my energy level drops. What little energy is left is spent on personal aggrandizement and selfish endeavors. I sincerely cannot imagine how some make it without reflectivity and prayer. In prayer I am reminded of my inadequacies and complete need for and dependence on the Supreme *Other.*

It is very easy for me to carp on trivialities when I do not pray. I think that when I do not pray I become self diverted. Prayer helps me to check excesses and to pay attention to what is really important. Prayer and reflection help me in self-work.

Social Support System: Paradoxically, it is easier to survive in Africa than in the developed world. Though surviving instinct is natural, I want to think that it takes time and efforts to learn surviving tactics. Family and community systems help to make survivability learned fast in Africa. The abundance of social amenities makes it more difficult to survive in the West. People in the developed world have become spoiled. In hard times, you hear about programs, talks, and workshops on how to become debt free, how to save, and how to do X, Y, Z of other money matters. I must confess that some of them are laudable programs. How about those persons who have lost so much that they have no money to save or manage? What do they talk about? What can we say to such people? As I said earlier, when extreme poverty strikes in our life every economic theory seems to fall apart at least for the individual. All we know is the stark reality of going downhill. The question I intend to ask here is, how can the poor be protected from economic downturn—even in America? We cannot deny reality for very long nor run away from it. When the recent economic recession began to creep into the global village, it was common among Nigerians to hear statements like, "We are okay. We do not have a credit system." That statement is now history. Yes! We are affected too. Even African countries with their comprehensive social support systems suffer in global economic turbulence. For them the hit could be very bad if not worse. The effect of globalization is real.

There are some avenues in developed countries that have not been explored as we try to solve the mesmerizing economic puzzle. We should not underrate the role of families, friends, and other social support networks. When we are rich we usually attract to ourselves as many as we allow of what I call "money-purchased friends." The story changes if we no longer have that money. The problem with being poor or loosing fame is that when we lose our money or fame we lose the business and social friends that having money or fame creates. We are left with families and few friends. The African proverb, "*When the corpse stinks, only the family is left to deal with it*" holds true here. By the way, what is wrong with us humans? We are seriously, helplessly, and pitifully trapped in this material world. Permit me to quote the bible in my personal language: "Blessed are those whose hearts are liberated from this world. Theirs is the kingdom of true happiness."

I believe the economic turbulence can be the cause of some positive things in American society. Unemployment causes some families to live together, reuniting them. Sharing can be enhanced. Our priorities are reordered. Only the truly essential metamorphose into. Hindsight is always 20/20—but it is never too late when we think a little more critically. I too have learned. There is no way I can make it without family and friends. I have learned from them spend more wisely. I have made responsible savings my goal. But I constantly remind myself that there is a fine line between savings and hoarding. The motive helps to clarify things. Love sharpens and clarifies the difference. I am not afraid to ask for help from friends and family. However I don't have to dangle my problems on the street or throw them in the face of my beloved. If I do that my neighbors, friend and family turn away from me. As we share joys and sorrows I try not to overwhelm my friends and families with mine.

People's problems are usually seen as simple by outsiders until they are asked to help. Sometimes, human beings do not see others' sufferings as a big issue until they enter the arena. Nonetheless we do not have to exaggerate our problems in order to attract attention to them. But be cautious. We don't want people to trivialize our issues either. That will make us less empowered than before. I am cautious when I listen to statements such as, "It's okay," "Stop lamenting," "You are not the only one," and "You are not the first person to go through this and you won't be the last." Sometimes people don't want to deal with us because they know we have problems. We should not be afraid. If they truly are friends and family, they will not be. If they are—maybe to have a break—they will always come back to embrace us. They know we are overwhelmed. They are probably working on how to help us. All we need to do is continue loving. I appreciate every single moment someone spends with me listening to my story.

Silence and Solitude: Our unspoken wisdom is like saving in the bank of our intelligence. Inside our cognitive world there should be no difference between our words and our wisdom. And this wisdom can only come from the Divine in us. The more we speak only when necessary and for the common good, the better our words become trained in their productivity. The more we do this the deeper we are drawn into the image and likeness of the Divine with us. Constant noise reduces our capacity for concentration which in turn makes us more uncomfortable with silence. It also reduces our energy level. Some people dread silence. Their reasons can be as numerous as there are excuses for noise. Silence forces us to think. If we do not try to drown its presence we are led to reflection and cognitive exercises. In the midst of constant noise I can develop migraine.

Silence is scary but also soothing. The human mind needs silence the way our body needs food. To live without silence, except when we are asleep, is like trying to drive a car without ever stopping at a gas station. The idea of finding time to move away from the noise of cars, engines, power sources, electricity, technological gadgets, etc., seems to be getting away from our generation. I do not consider the voice of nature or other humans as noise. These natural voices sound in our ears when there is a need to attend to positive power, energy and force within or outside us. I do not consider them to be noise. If you pay attention and think deeper, sincerely speaking, they are not. As a matter of fact, I must attend to them. Sometimes I want to believe I need them to survive. The voice of the other in a relationship, the sound of rain, the songs of birds and insects, the bleating of goats, the meow of cats, the barking of dogs are all the symbiotic orchestration of harmony required by humans to maintain the celestial homeostasis needed for terrestrial equilibrium. The African woman in the village has plenty of this.

Authority: We need to move back to what was in order to capture what might have been. We need to use our past to capture the future in the present. We have discussed the topic of authority in Chapters 6 and 7. Even though they may seem powerless, African women have inbuilt authority. I know my authority. My authority lies in my ability to love and care. I am fully human when I love. Love is hardwired in us. When we do not love our very nature is thwarted. Then we may be out-of-touch with our Source of authority and a lot can go wrong.

Collective Feminism: When an African woman stands alone she is at a loss; she is powerless and loses all the strength. But in a group an African woman finds her voice and her power. Her song is sweeter and her voice is more melodious in a group. Her community is her power when she believes that what she is about is for the good of her children. She wants to protect the land and its customs.

African Women celebrate love and joy at meal time: courtesy of Ethiopian Diamond Broadway, Chicago

She is Mother Earth in a way that doesn't allow you to trample her. You can try but we do not forget that she holds our gravity and her authority is unquestionable.

In many African societies, men who fear that their women may become empowered do not allow their wives or partners to join a feminist group. Many people have asked for my opinion on African feminism. I always replied, "What is feminism?" I ask this because I want to understand their perception about feminism. We cannot meet someone halfway if we do not know where she or he is coming from. There are as many understandings of African feminism as there are people who have asked. Education and economic strength are the best means of empowerment for African women. Yet these are dreaded by some African men. They fear competition from women in business. At times they seem to engage in an unconscious but substantial monopoly of certain businesses, professions and other sectors of the economy. Their excuse is that women cannot do it. I believe they are probably afraid that women in positions of authority will expose men's weaknesses, corruption, inefficiency and irresponsibility. When we were growing up I remember irresponsible drivers dreading women police more than anything. Commercial drivers would park for hours when they found out there was a female police officer at the checkpoint ahead. Today, one rarely sees female police officers at the checkpoints. Female police officers are leaving the profession out of the frustration at not being promoted.

One challenge which feminism in Africa faces is that those who engage in it are those who are already liberated. They include African women who have a good education such as those with bachelors, masters degrees or even doctorate; professionals like lawyers, professors, doctors and businesses women including sophisticated entrepreneurs. Feminism is an issue discussed in classrooms, conferences and other academic forums. There is no African word for feminism. For the African woman feminism is not a theory or a practice. It is a movement. Like any movement, it happens. It exists out of necessity. It is born when a group of women experience so much injustice they are driven to do something about it. In Africa feminism rises up when women face death and they believe they must act. They find themselves up against the wall and there is no escape unless they push back. This causes feminism to emerge.

The problem is that many African women, for the most part, have not articulated the many socio-cultural injustices and human rights violations meted out to them and their children.

I remember one Sister who told us a story when I was in secondary school. It was about an American missionary who became very angry about the way men were treating their wives. The missionary complained to the parish priest, hoping to receive his support and approval for a renewed mission project which she termed "feminism for Christ." She was kicked out of the village the following day, not by the men but by the women. What happened, she found out later, was that the parish priest had called all the men in the village to an emergency meeting to warn them about what the missionary was intending to do. He exaggerated the missionary's intentions to the point the men thought they would be overthrown by their wives if they allowed the missionary to go ahead with her plans. So the men went home and warned their wives of the impending doom. The women took over the war against the missionary and drove her out of the village.

How did the women come to look at Ms. Missionary with such suspicion? They must have entertained thoughts such as, "She is not one of us," "She doesn't understand us," "She doesn't even speak our language," and "She doesn't look like us." Consequently, the women did not trust her intentions. The men, the priest, and the women all had different reasons for driving the missionary out of the village. Today I believe things have changed. But still, many African women, more than African men, do not want to hear about feminism. There is this identifiable fear in many African women and some African men when the feminism is mentioned.

Feminism has negative connotation on African soil. Feminism is so hated by traditional women that one carefully avoids the use of the term when doing women organizing. African feminists are looked down upon. Those who engage in feminist activities are subjected to name calling and labeling, such as "women who want to become men," "wives who want to become the head of the family," "they want to marry their husbands instead of husbands marrying them," "they have learned to wear trousers, pretty soon they will begin to climb palm trees," and so on. What the African woman needs is human rights awareness and education in social justice. Awareness programs are critically needed in women organizing. An African woman needs to see the injustices and the abuses in her community. She has to first acknowledge and accept that things are not right before she can work to make them right. She does not need to be told that things are not right. You cannot tell an African woman that something is wrong with her culture and tradition. She will mistrust you and refuse to work with you even when she needs you. She is the custodian of her culture and traditions. Her society knows that without her and her children, its culture and traditions would not be what they are. The big question here is, "How does one help an African woman see that some things are not right in her culture or tradition?" The mission of AfWiAm tries to address this question.

Elasticity and Flexibility: The more materially comfortable we become the lower our threshold for suffering. The more I pass through pains and difficulties, the more flexible and emotionally elastic I become. My endurance has been trained through the abuses and victimizations in my life. The need for survival and continued struggles to keep my head above the water force me to bounce back. It is as if I have been trained in the art of suffering. One of my American friends who has visited Africa once joked, "NG, do you know that if one-tenth of the suffering in Africa was transferred to America all of us here would die within a few days?"

Let us consider two kinds of stress: facilitating and debilitating. Facilitating stress is the normal, regular stress that makes me want to get out of bed. It is this stress that helps me be up and doing. On the other hand, the killer stress is that which arises from things that are calling for urgent attention within limited time or resources. Sometimes, debilitating stress can emanate from faulty or broken systems and structures. It can arise from the malfunctioning of structures or infrastructures. When someone does not do her or his duty, others in the community feel the effects. I call this *organized stress* because it stems from an organized society. It can also arise from an organizational malfunctioning and irresponsibility. Oftentimes it is not possible to escape organized stress.

An unorganized stress is present most often in disorganized societies. In this type of society everyone is doing what he or she likes. There seems to be lawlessness and disorder. People are not held accountable for their corrupt practices and misbehaviors. From top to bottom, no one seems to be responsible for offenders. There is an unorganized stress in this type of system. In this case, stress can be avoided at all cost—*hakuna matata,* translated as "there are no worries." After all, no one holds anyone accountable and no one brings the offenders to justice. Paradoxically, this is a pitiable situation. Members in societies where there is less law and order learn to shield themselves from stress since no one protects them from the lawless offenders. They build a kind of elasticity and flexibility that will help them escape dangers when sensed.

The more organized a society the greater its tendency to make demands on its citizens to maintain the organized structure. It reaches a point when it seems like things have been inverted. Instead of the structure being organized for humans, humans become organized for the structure. People find themselves stifled by a straightjacket of stringent and rigid rules and regulations. The good news is that none of these is permanent. I believe humans are imbued with a natural harmony. If this is allowed to develop and grow, obeying law and order will not be as stressful as they are to some people. Some people struggle to comply with the rules and regulations of their daily lives even after years of being subjected to them. That is why many suffer stress-related illnesses. But we should not feel too bad. It is consoling to remember that no one suffers from stress alone although some are affected more than others. When someone is stressed or depressed, all the neighbors, friends, family, the job, and the people at the workplace all feel it. It is infectious.

Even the earth is becoming stressed by pollution, climate change, loss of bio-diversity, etc. The environmental stress affects heaven and all of us. But together we can use our endowed gifts of adaptability to help. We should learn to live within the harmony of nature as we deal with self, others, and the environment. We need to treat fellow humans and our environment with great respect. As a mother, I want to be sure the earth is heard as she cries. The earth lives and breathes just like you and me. We should not exploit it anyway we like and attempt to control it for our own materialistic desires. If we do not respect and care for Mother Earth she will revolt because it is in her nature to do so. Emotional elasticity and docility help us to help us to stay afloat as well as deal with the environment responsibly. Take swimming for example. We can't float free if we don't let go. Resilience, relaxation, buoyancy, and freedom allow for free floating. The more we want to control the harder it is to be free. If we insist, we become stressed or depressed.

The lighter we are with life, the lesser the pain of our brokenness. One of the women in a rural village of Togo shared a very interesting story that kept us laughing for five minutes. Elise was my interpreter since my French is not so good. She said, *"A group of men had gone to a marriage party. My husband attended the party even though he wasn't invited. Wherever there is free booze, there you will see my husband. When it was over he joined his friends to go back. There was no space for some of them except in the back of an open truck. Everyone in and on the truck was drunk except Francois. They were all singing and acting stupid when the driver lost control. The truck started to somersault eyewitnesses said, and one by one, they were all jettisoned. They all survived except Monsieur Francois – the only sober person in the group, who died on the spot. (the husband was among those who survived) I believe my husband survived because he was so drunk he probably did not know what was happening. They probably thought they were acrobats."* The group rolled into laughter maybe at the word 'acrobats'. I missed the joke due to cultural contextual difference.. "Since that day, I no longer bother my husband when he comes home drunk," she concluded. This story is shared to argue the point that suggests we break when we are too perfect and too rigid. When we allow for some flexibility and enough room for space where we could laugh at ourselves, then we can bounce back more readily and more easily when life becomes tough.

Exercise and Recreation: Walking, song and dance, folklore while sitting by the fireside, stories and laughter, domestic duties—farming, fetching firewood, drawing water, carrying her baby on her back—plus all the other family and community formal ceremonies help extend our adaptability. Physical and spiritual exercises train and trim my mind and body. I used to walk a lot. I think I stopped walking when I came to America. I want to start walking more. When I walk, I use less gas and save the Earth for the future generation. It also makes me healthy and whole. I seize every opportunity that knocks at my door to get in as much walking as I can in a day.

I tease my friends who drive all the time. We have two legs; our car has four. Using the four tires costs us more money and adds extra pounds of weight to our legs. Using our legs saves us money and makes us look sweet. We take the car everywhere we go. We even take the car to someone's facility. We park the car and walk into her or his office. After some paperwork, we pay the person to walk out of his or her facility. I love America—the country of my dreams—but I still don't understand why we waste so much money. One of my professors at Loyola University Chicago captured it vividly when he said that while we become sick and die from excess in America, people become sick and die from scarcity in Africa.

◆

CHAPTER ELEVEN
They Rule, We Lead

The Woman: In her being and terms is the inclusive language, yet she is excluded in many things. Man in wo-man, he in s-he, male in fe-male. But who accepts it? At this point, some of you are probably thinking, *Here she goes again, crazy as always.* Please, before you think I am crazy, remember we (women) are difficult to understand because we have neither language nor vocabulary. We don't have words formed from letters. We are truly sophisticated. If you don't understand, that proves what I say. To make her submissive they tie numbers around her and use words formed from letters to describe her. Science and arts are human inventions meant to control time and space. That is not a bad thing. As a matter of fact, it is awesome to imagine the beautiful and great things science and art have contributed to human improvement. But when science and art are used to label some better than others it is unfair. It is crime when science and art are used abuse women and children. It is evil.

I want to believe the inventors of science and arts intended good. It does not always work because science and art are partial and imperfect; they are explorations by limited humans of the Creator's unlimited creations. But we keep trying. The presence of womanhood in the world continues to remind us that our universe is vast but our knowledge is limited. The woman has not lost her authority. That should give the world some consolation.

The 2008 Women's Leadership Conference at Loyola University Chicago (http://www.luc.edu/womensleadership/Event_Women's_Leader) provided me with more tools for my mission with African women. I walked away from that conference with a few statements that have grounded my beliefs. (1) *Men see opportunities, women see risks.* (2) *Allow for certain levels of vulnerability.* (3) *People don't care how much you know about them; they know how much you care.* (4) *Don't make excuses; make efforts.* I want to believe that women think with their heart. I don't want to sound sexist but I also think men tend to feel with their head. Whether this is part of the male nature or not is not the issue here. The question is, "What do we do with how we think and feel?" It does not help to try to be like one gender or the other; otherwise it can be limiting.

Circle of Life: Growing up in a girls' boarding school, the common slogan when faced with difficult tasks was, "What a man can do, a woman can do—even better." This slogan helped us accomplish a lot in school. It led us to compete vigorously in sports and academics with all the surrounding boys' schools. Our physical strength seemed to be insurmountable when there was no man around. Upon graduation, many of us got married. Little by little the women began to surrender their physical strength. Before long they became fulltime housewives. All that power and even her unique authority was handed over to the husband the day she said, "I do." Unfortunately she received none of her husband's powers as the rings were being exchanged. It was a one-way flow of power. From then on the husbands become the rulers.

The husband turns himself into a god when the woman's authority is surrendered completely and absolutely. That is dangerous. We are still mere humans. If men presume they are gods, they must remember women are goddesses. Then there will be mutual respect and honor. You hear very many African women helplessly lament about the cruelty and injustice they suffer at the hands of their husbands. They have been dependent on their husbands so long that they have forgotten how to be independent and self-supporting. They are not even codependent on each other. The thoughts of losing their husbands scare the hell out of African women. Some of these women spend more time caring for their husbands than for their children and themselves. How noble and life-giving this caring would be if done out of love rather than the fear of losing her partner.

The husband fears the authority of the woman and of losing her servitude. The woman fears the power of the man. The children live in constant fear of being battered and are frightened by the verbal abuse exchanged by their parents. The house is full of people living and being raised in fear. When they grow up, the children will imitate what they are experiencing and observing. The circle continues, unbroken. If you suggest to some African men that it might be good for their wives to have as much prowess with money as they do, they will label you a feminist and a destroyer of families. They will caution their wives not to associate with you.

Some African women have become so caught up in dependency that their husbands work themselves like slaves. In their over-controlling attitude and ego protection, African men slave themselves to death. In the end both have been cheated and the children suffer the consequences. The African proverb, "When two elephants fight the grass suffers" is on the money here. Many African men die prematurely. I come from a culture that has twenty widows for every widower. The widower quickly remarries as the culture expects. So there is no widower, so to speak. On the other hand, a widow who remarries, especially after having a male child, is looked upon with contempt. In both the short and long run, everyone, particularly the women and children, suffer the consequences of a unidirectional flow of power.

The Ultimate Fear: One of my friends, and a priest for that matter (I know a few that are a little crazy), said there are three groups that feel threatened by women's talents and gifts and will do anything to protect their positions of power: "African men, the Catholic church, and the Muslim religion." "Bingo!" I responded. "Please tell this to the appropriate officials," I chimed. Only autocrats fear power sharing. Leadership does not. The concept of leadership is different from being a named leader. The fact that one is called the *leader* of a group does not necessarily mean that the person will exercise true leadership. The essence of something is much more than the name we hang on it. So it is with how we label or denote womanhood and her position in society. Recall that the reason we name people and things is for recognition and identification, not understanding. My name is Ngozichukwu (*Blessing of the Great Chi*). No one, including myself can totally understand who I am. You could equally write a book on the phrase "Blessing of the Great Chi" and still not be able to neither exhaust its meaning or tell adequately who I am. So when some speak of themselves as a leader of a group, it sometimes comes across to me that the better word is *ruler.*

Leadership is a head-heart practice. It is a virtue and only a few have it. Those in power are often mistaken to be leaders. To describe oneself as a leader means that there is a process or movement in which someone is at a described in which he or she does the same thing that all in the group do and follow the same direction that all in the group follow. The leader illustrates what needs to be done by her or his living example. We know from experience this is not always the case. A position of power can mean one is directing, presiding, executing, ordering, commanding, adjudicating, or umpiring but does not necessarily mean leading. This position sets one apart from the rest. That can be called rulership. In light of this description, I can say that the majority of African societies are under the rulership of men. Many African women are under the rulership of their husbands. They decide and tell us what to do. For instance, in many cases women have little or no say in the economic life and principle affairs of the family.

Because the man plays the pipe he dictates the tune. In many cases, many women have shared their fears with me. "Because my husband is a dictator in the economic life of the family, he misses so much in what I have to offer. I feel consumed by the fire of my gifts and talents because I cannot share them with my family," she laments. In some cases I meet with the men, and some of their responses are: "Am I holding her back?" "She is a child and does not know what she is saying." "If she wants to be the boss I will come home and take care of the children and she can go out there and be the man." "I don't know what is wrong with women." "Women are insatiable; what is her problem? I provide her with everything she needs." And when I asked these men, "What if you die?" some quickly retorted, "Sister, do you want to kill me?" "Not yet." Some others laughed the question off. Back to commenting on their wives some grumbled, "Let her wait till I die unless she wants to kill me." It goes on and on. My question is, What is at the root of these threats and fear? I will consider this question in my following work, *African Women and the Psychology of Oppression.*

The imagination of an African woman is not directed to conquest. Her dream is to live. Love empowers her authority. That is why her quest is to lead, not rule. Hence dwelling in the past is not imperative for an African woman. Otherwise she will burn in the fire of the constant evils as she reflects on the unjust experiences and daily abuses of her dignity. She passes through all these for the sake of her children. She lets them pass.

She forgives. She understands that when she does not forgive her offender she is holding him in the jail of her heart. Neither she nor her offender is free. This can drain her physically. But she needs her energy in order to continue leading even though her leadership is not recognized. She knows she is at the center of circle or life and hope for her children. All she asks is a space to share her leadership qualities.

Without claims of being a sleep specialist there are some things I have observed from personal experiences. When my sleep patterns change and I begin to find it difficult to sleep, some simple self-evaluative questions expose where I am and what I do. If I notice I am sleeping more than usual, I know there is a problem. When sleeping problems occur in my life and it is not connected to illness or medication, it could be due to living too much in my head or too much in my heart. When it results from living in my head more than in the heart I will suffer from sleep deprivation. When it results from too much living in my heart, there will be too much sleepiness.

I don't think humans are created to live too much in the head or too much in the heart. Humans are made capable of extraordinary love and care and that can be done with head-heart intelligence. We have a right and a duty to expect leadership from those placed at the head of affairs among people or in society. When people fear instead of love, they do not obey out of love. They do not see any intrinsic value in the law and order. They obey out of habit or because they do not want to face the consequence of disobedience. That seems to be the type of fear in the rulership and followership present in Africa. That's unfortunate.

Love that Heals and Builds: Leadership brings healing to the people being led. In my Clinical Pastoral Education (CPE) class there was so much emphasis on feeling it seemed we being trained to feel but not think. We cannot feel as humans without our mind or our reasoning. These mental faculties help us to check excesses of emotional outbursts. We forget that human emotions are mental products which show through feelings. Our emotions and our minds are inseparable whether we are in touch with their operations or not.

I tried to explain my stand on that issue for months since my peers believed I am all head. Finally, it fell out of my lips: "You know, when emotions are at work, reasoning goes on vacation." It is very difficult to reason when you are in an emotional state. For instance, someone immersed in grief over the loss of a friend does not remember that there are many other friends yet to be made. It happened to me when I lost one of my dear friends, Fr. Patrick Nnabuife, to a fatal auto accident. Initially, I did not want my reasoning to travel; my reasoning was "in charge" of me throughout the funeral and burial ceremonies. I did not allow myself to feel until after his burial. Then when I allowed myself to feel, I lost all rationalization. I allowed my emotions to overwhelm me. I became so sick that I lost ten pounds in two days. I was buried in deep mourning for the loss of my friend. I began to feel better the minute I began to reason. I began to say, "I miss you, but it is okay to let you go. I love you dearly. You are beautifully irreplaceable, but there is much other irreplaceable beauty hanging around the world. Let me reach out to them because the clock is ticking. Love is being wasted. I let you go, friend. Adieu, dear!" I am not trying to dismiss the pain of loss. What I am saying is that the mourner must come to accept these statements. Once these cogno-affective statements begin to inform our mourning, we begin to feel better. Also, time heals. The mourner must come to own this reasoning. It does not help when someone else supplies them. Once the mourner begins to reason again, one of two things must have happened. Either the emotions have dropped sufficiently so that the reasoning that went on vacation could return, or the emotions dropped entirely, making room for reason to sit on its throne once again.

When humans were created, we were expected to reason and feel simultaneously, not one or the other. Love is when we feel heartily with our reason and we think reasonably with our heart. The authority bestowed on humans lies in our ability to love. Lower animals such as the pets can also love. But human love is uniquely different and sophisticatedly beautiful because we are made in the image and likeness of our Creator. If there is any ruler, it is the Creator. But from the dawn of civilization man has consistently considered himself the ruler of the woman and the child.

It seems human invention reached its peak in the twentieth century. Humans constantly improve and enhance these inventions. But if we continue to invent and develop without head-heart intelligence, we are bound to have another Tower of Babel. We are bound to go to war and invent weapons of mass destruction and weapons of individual destruction. Love is the Creator's unique mark on humans. Although this mark of godliness in humans is bequeathed to us at conception it does not come automatically. It is learned. It is developed as a virtue or given as a gift. Like all divine gifts, leadership is given for others. If learned it is for the benefit of those led. Whether as a divine gift or developed as a virtue it is learned through discipline and sacrifice. It is the same with leadership. Leadership, like love, is either given or learned for the benefit of those led.

Leading with Head-Heart Intelligence: Leadership comes by using the head and the heart together. Leadership devoid of love is rulership. With the head alone it becomes the kind of leadership a machine or computer could provide. When it is with the heart alone it becomes very erotic, emotional, sentimental, and selective about who to love and who not to love. Everything can go wrong when the one at the helm leads without head-heart intelligence. Once it tastes leadership, a society never wants to go back to rulership. There are limits to human tolerance on rulership. People use all means to find leadership. They seek justice and liberation. They long for true leadership.

This longing is more apparent in the developed world than in developing nations. Quite often they use peaceful demonstrations and strikes. In extreme cases they revolt. Rulership pushes those ruled to the limit. When they reach that limit it becomes their strength which they use to push back and they cry out: "We want leadership. We are fed up with rulership."

When someone has neither experienced suffering and hardship nor known someone closely who has experienced these crosses it is very difficult for such a person to lead at all, much less be a good leader. The person can at least be a ruler. Love makes leadership possible. Might only realizes rulership.

CHAPTER TWELVE
They Have Power, We Have Authority

I always tell people I am not so much as ambitious as I want to achieve. I believe the sky is not a limit but a beginning. I believe the same for everybody else. I have a different definition of *the sky*. People look up when you ask them to point to the sky. For me the sky is the universe and *all* it contains, visible and invisible. Love and authority are wings on which we soar into a limitless sky. Love empowers authority. Only love can give a life and healthy functionality to authority. Authority is service-oriented. If someone has power but does not have love, one cannot truly serve and therefore cannot say she or he has true authority. This authority is liberating for the one holding it as well as those for whom is it held. It is used for the good of the people served. One who holds power may occasionally feel threatened, but the one who has authority fears not. Love enables one to soar like an eagle. It helps us dream of the impossible and achieve it.

Usually our Maker shows us a lot in our instinct, perception, or dream if we pay attention to the divine inspirations in us. I had some of the strangest dreams of my life, some of which I am reluctant to share, even with my friends. Once I dreamed there was a gathering of men to discuss how the village work would be shared. In the dream I believed I had something to contribute. There were no women in the gathering. In fact, all the women were returning and the men were going in my direction. All the women who passed me looked at me like I was out of my mind. At one point, shortly before I reached the venue, I stood there and grew myself a *john thomas*. Now how would I prove to the men that I had one? They might still kick me out of the meeting. I decided to go anyway. Should any of them doubt me I would go to a corner of the bushes where they could see me, take out my *JT*, and begin to pee. No one asked me to leave the meeting and I was the only woman from the beginning of the gathering to the end. Dreams like this usually reveal the other side of my hidden self. I will explore other mysterious dreams in my forthcoming spiritual autobiography *The Mystery of a Calling*.

During the time I was actualizing my authority I had a lot of recurring dreams. I believe this was because I was venturing into that inward me where I would be more readily conscious of the CHINEKE. I frequently dream of flying. The first time I shared this dream, I was told to never say it in public because only witches and wizards have dreams of flying. But in my dreams my flights saved a lot of people who were in danger. In my dreams, I have received many revelations about impending doom or dangers in my waking life. It took me decades to embrace this dreaming self. As I look back on it, I can testify that I was being drawn by the loving hearts of our Lord Jesus Christ and His Blessed Virgin Mother Mary. Their love made it possible for me.

The Christ in Me: I became so greatly enamored of Christ's authority in me that once I embraced His love, fear lost its grip on me. I began to soar even higher. I became more and more detached from the earth and many things became less important to me. I became lighter and was enabled to fly to greater heights. Like I shared earlier, when one of the bishops I worked with in Nigeria said to me one day, "Why are you not afraid to speak when others dread coming to us?" I answered that

I am only afraid of someone who is not a servant or a child of God. Love makes me fearless. I can take any risk as long as it is done out of love. I repeat, we cannot err if we love in every venture. If I am not afraid to talk with BAMBA, who is almighty, if I hold great conversations with ALLAH, and then I should not be afraid to speak with the Creator's children or mere servants. I have a tremendous fear of associating with anyone I believe is neither a child nor a servant of God. Being afraid of someone does not mean I do not love them. But I may not associate with them as freely as I would if I was assured by their actions or words that they are God's child or servant. I think that if we believe in the same principles and strive to live a life of love, we share authority. The more love a person has the more authority she or he has. The reason the Supreme Being has absolute authority over humanity and all that exists is because God is love and love is God.

CHAPTER THIRTEEN
The Lost Innocence in the Land

They Harmed Our Harmony: In the land of the Igbo people as in many other African cultures, there were rules and regulations regarding how and when to fetch water. It was a sacred ritual with great respect for the land. Everybody abided by the code. The Genesis account states that the world was created in six days. The seventh day was hallowed by Yahweh, obligating humans to also rest and hallow that day. This was for the honor of the Creator but also for the health of humans. The Igbo people have four days in a week. One of these days is sacred and must be a day of rest after devoting three days to acquiring what is needed. Different Igbo societies have a different day of rest.

These four days are *Eke, Orie, Afo,* and *Nkwo.* Before the Europeans came to the land, Africans lived by simple basic rules that acknowledged human rights. Certain fundamental human rights existed before the arrival of the Europeans. The Igbo people are traditionally very religious and down-to-earth. Wisdom and African traditional religion preserved peace and harmony and fostered the social and economic lives of individual communities. Bodies of water such as ponds, streams, rivers, lakes, oceans, and seas are considered fundamental human rights given to them by CHUKWU. They were respected. People did not just do whatever they liked with and in these water bodies. The early Europeans violated these rights and consequently taught the people how to. Then they turned around and spoke of fundamental human rights. I think it became confusing to my people. We were very healthy and hearty. With a very few terminal illnesses, people's lifespans were a hundred years or more. The food, drink, and lifestyle were natural and organic. Looking back it is apparent that the first visitors to the African land did not to do so well. Let me share a story with you. The names are fictitious but the story is true.

There was the River Dum in Nneato village and the village celebrated Nkwo as their holy day of obligation. On Nkwo, no one went to the River Dum. Masquerades (occult group of men [rarely women] who mask themselves and are believed to rely extensively on the use of African science in their activities. They depend on charms, amulets, and rituals believed to provide them with power and immunity from human harm and danger. Among the Igbo, masquerades are said to be spirits. Their name, *muonwu—spirits from the dead*—is coined from the belief that they are spirits, not human) *and youths would stand guard in the river's forest and at the riverbanks. Although violators were rare they were usually dealt with seriously when caught.*

There are three seasons in the year: dry, rainy and harmattan. During the dry and harmattan seasons, women and youth go to the river more frequently.

So, on Eke, the first day of the week for the Nneato people, all the families in the community and neighboring towns would go to fetch drinking water. Elders who had no young person in their family would be cared for by others. Only drinking water was fetched on the Eke day. Everyone would collect enough drinking water for the next three days—Orie, Afo, and Nkwo.

On Orie, families would go to fetch water from the River Dum for domestic needs such as cooking and watering the animals. The people fetched enough to meet their domestic needs for the next three days.

On Afo, they went down to the river to do their laundry.

On Nkwo, the holiday of obligation, no one went to the river. The river would be peaceful and undisturbed for twenty-four hours, clean and ready for fetching drinking water on Eke.

Almost every evening except on Nkwo, people would go to the river take a bath, swim, and have fun. The women and children's quarters would be at the source of the river and the men's would be downriver. If a woman or a child had a mishap upstream the men could come to the rescue before they were carried away by the currents.

This was an example of the way people maintained rules and regulation concerning the use of bodies of water. It helped them maintain good health and proper hygiene. When the Europeans came they introduced Western democracy, which was different from the democracy that existed. "Freedom all the way," they proclaimed. It was free land, free water, free time, free speech, and free *everything*. The people knew their freedom stopped only where ONYE OKIKE's absoluteness began. The Europeans went to the river whenever they liked. They encouraged the people to do the same. They disrupted the established law and order. Out of respect, the masquerades and the youth did not harm them. "Ojemba enwe iro"—"a traveler (visitor) has no enemy"—is a treasured proverb for travelers. The visitors probably told them they would stink if they did not bathe every day. So the villagers went to the river anytime on any day. The missionaries meant well. Their work was accomplished, but the people of the land paid the price.

Mama Sophia picks up the challenge by African children: Stephanie Toman Secretary, Travis Proffitt co-founders of AfWiAm and the children watch as Mama Sophia helps a young African girl carry her water up the hill.

The early Europeans taught the people to pay no attention to the law of the land. As a matter of fact, there was no law (so they thought) since all people were labeled *pagans. P*eople started to suffer untold diseases. Typhoid, diarrhea, and other waterborne diseases became prevalent. The water had become polluted. People started getting sick from drinking from the river. When natural harmony, social order, and community law are broken, humans and other living things suffer the consequences. The land lost its innocence and the people paid the price. Later missionaries worked hard to correct some of these damages but we know from experience it is easier to tear down and rebuild than try to fix the problem.

CHAPTER FOURTEEN
The Missionary

The 'Mary Magdalene and Paul' in Us: When you meet someone for the first time there is nothing that immediately suggests whether they are good or bad. Hopefully all we see is beauty and the Creator's signature of love. That is what my religion taught me. When we meet people we should see a life-giving mark in them. Their Maker's mark of ownership should be written on their foreheads. We should see the beauty of the image and likeness of the Supreme Being. Only when the person says or does something can we begin to assess where the person belongs or predict where they are going. We begin to ponder whose missionary she or he is. Women seem to have a knack for doing this pondering more accurately and better than men.

Some of the questions we should ask when we go on mission are, "What can we do together, the citizens and the missionaries?" "How can we empower each other?" "What does development mean in this mission land," and "What are some of the long-term effects of our presence in this land?" We know that the earliest missionaries to Africa made a lot of incorrect assumptions about the people, many mistakes regarding the land, and some blunders in their mission strategies. We want to believe their motives were not insidious. We readily excused them, saying they were doing their best. Nonetheless, I think some of them made costly mistakes, such as asking us to "throw away the baby with the bathwater." They asked us to throw away our roots and some of our precious traditions because they labeled everything paganism. We forgave them. We have not stopped excusing them. Maybe because we know we are not any better. Men have built their own unjust practices on their legacy, all in the name of religion. These excuses have caused us to lose much that is beautiful. This costly mistake has made it difficult for true Christianity to take root in the soil and hearts of Africans. It has also made it difficult for genuine twenty-first century missionaries to be effective because they are finding it difficult to write straight on crooked lines. They cannot easily correct those early mistakes and the Church is paying for it. It is quite difficult to find pure and authentic Christianity in Africa.

Even some of the present day missionaries pretend to be true Christians. But love has no part in their plans or projects. When they develop projects they are more interested in what will yield them money and a good number of sycophants. They target the very rich for money and the very poor for easy indoctrination.

Let us be humble enough to start all over. Let us pray to God, who trusted a woman that the Word became incarnate in her womb. Let us pray to Jesus of Nazareth, who, after he rose from the dead, entrusted the mission to women when he said, "Go and tell my disciples that I am alive." A religion becomes rooted in the life of the people when women are involved. Sometimes it seems religious leaders forget that women are the Earth. When seeds are planted on the earth and she is fertile, they grow into hundred folds. Their roots are deep and strong, and their branches become widespread.

Their Arrival: There was community in Africa before Christianity or Islam came. I am from Igbo-Ukwu, an archeological city in Eastern Nigeria. Igbo-Ukwu is a predominantly Christian town. I remember when growing up in the 1970s the last African traditional religion (ATR) worshipper in my village died. After his death the shrine he attended became obsolete. At that time there were only the Catholic and Anglican churches. The Cherubim and Seraphim (a spiritual Christian group) was despised and labeled a cult. Now many people are going back to ATR or joining any of the new Pentecostal churches, their reason being they have not found the love they expected to find in the Christian church. The factions, cold war, and hatred among Catholics, Anglicans, other Christian denominations, and non-Christians are more serious now than what existed between Christians and Pagans in the town when the first missionaries arrived. If Christianity was rooted in the hearts of my people, the young people would not have lost their faith and zest so fast. All the divisions, ill will, and conflict plaguing that town would not have existed if the early Christian missionaries had built on the love and community present when they arrived. The effects of their missionary endeavors were apparently temporary. You might call it a transient Christianity. It bloomed in the morning of evangelization. But then the sun shined on it and it could not survive the heat. Now is afternoon and it is dying. Some may think the African church is still prospering. Yes, but only when you compare it to the European or American churches. People are living in hatred and fear of one another. All trust is gone. Do we need re-evangelization? Yes! I believe we can re-mission effectively if we first humble ourselves before the Creator of us all. We need to surrender to the Master of the Missions—Jesus Himself—and pray that He resends us with a new spirit and a new approach. The woman in me believes it is not too late.

What are the purposes of modern-day missionaries? To develop programs and projects that generate sustainable and long-lasting spiritual and material development? Initiate programs that continue to thrive and benefit the natives after the missionaries are gone? Ensure their projects emancipate and empower rather than keep people dependent on them? Model and sow the seeds of love for which Christ came? Or ensure their projects and programs die as soon as they leave the land so that it would continue to look like Africans cannot help themselves? I do not want to overwhelm you with rhetorical questions, but these are some that trouble the minds of many Africans, women more than men. I know two religious communities in East Africa that do not want to recruit promising candidates. Their reason is best known to them. But I can argue with information available that it is because they do not want people who might outshine them. The question here is, do their efforts promote sustainability *for* the mission or sustainability *as* a missionary? It is amazing how a phrase can twist a mission's purpose. I encourage missionaries of all types—diplomats, religious, investors, and entrepreneurs, as well as adventurers and explorers—to be courageous enough to establish and develop sustainable programs in their mission lands. When the people no longer need us, let us be humble enough to decrease so that they may increase. We can visit friends we have made. We can also go to our former missionary fields as tourists to enjoy a job well done.

Some of the African religious leaders are not any better. Sometimes I fear that religious leaders may have lost the vision. For instance, when I look at what is happening in some African Christian churches, it is disheartening. It is sad to observe that some of those colonial strategies, such as "divide and conquer," "conquer to rule," "keep them blind," "partition of Africa," and "survival of the fittest" have been adopted by African religious leaders. They are so determined to protect the institutions, systems, and structures they have erected even at the pain of losing the flock. If one member leaves the church it is not a big deal, especially if he is not a financial backbone of the parish. The woman in me can no longer keep silent. I am hurting because I believe the Mother Church is hurting.

I hurt when I see injustice and corruption happen in the church that is my Mother. I know I share in these evils, but I am powerless. I am a woman, but I am a mother. I am the Earth. That is why I must cry. Like the proverbial mother hen, *I am not crying so that our predators let go of their grips on my children; I am crying so that the world may hear my voice.*

I am a missionary to African women. I have to think that my recent AfWiAm visit to West Africa did much more for me than for the rural women I visited. My twenty-two days of just being with the rural women did more than just open my eyes. They changed me forever. My mind and feelings are grounded in what is important in life and what needs to be attended to. The visits have helped me to reevaluate myself as an African woman and a missionary in the world. They have helped me to ask over and over, "Why was I created? Why am I a woman? Why am I an African? What is my purpose on earth as a child of the global village? How can I make a real and lasting difference in the lives of fellow humans, particularly other women and children?" These questions have helped me become more reflective. They also help me maintain the requisite humility needed for any twenty-first century worthwhile mission endeavors.

Kinds of Mission: Humans are made beautifully strong. The Creator endowed us humans with reasoning and responsible common sense. I argue that women are still the builders of any community or society even though humans may run it down. You and I believe that everyone wants to be part of a community or group. We also want to live and thrive. What we do not know is that our power to live and thrive happily lies hidden in our power to love. These constitute the essence of the authority we hold as humans. As I articulated above, we are all missionaries on earth—whether we believe it or not—and no missionary succeeds without great love.

We are all missionaries on earth in various shapes or forms. There are diplomatic, religious, business, and social missionaries. There are also adventurers and explorers. Let me make an assertion here. There is a difference between a soldier and a missionary. The soldiers' love for their country sustains them while the missionary is sustained by love for the country to which they are sent. Christian missionaries are sustained by their love modeled by Jesus of Nazareth, who gave His life for the people to whom He was sent.

Both the soldier and the missionary must try to make a positive and indelible impact on the land to which they are sent while bringing home the trophy. We are YAHWEH's soldiers here on earth embattled in the war between evil and good, between principalities and powers. The love of God who sends us empowers all we do. It also sustains us. We are also missionaries here on earth. We must love all the children of the earth. Our love for the Creator and others, in response to the divine love, carries us through. Grace makes our work possible, either as a soldier or as a missionary.

When people are on a mission and are serious about it, they don't take pictures. This is because if they do, they are either journalists or spies, not soldiers. No soldier in his or her right mind stops to take pictures in the heat of the battle. Every conscious missionary is constantly on a battlefield. The mission land is a battlefield. When one is busy in the missions, one has neither the time nor the desire to take pictures. Missionaries do not need to prove what they are doing. The people whose lives they touch are the proof. People ask me what makes African women trust me enough that they are willing and ready to share some of their most secret and perturbing experiences. My answer is, "When people see love, care, and concern, they know. If these women see love they know it. If they know love they trust and with trust they are ready to open up like flowers and pour out."

CHAPTER FIFTEEN
African Women and Religion

The Dance of Goddesses: *They are African women. They dance and dance until their sorrows become washed away by the river of sweat on their brows. These Mother Earths clap hands in a rhythmic fashion. Their voices and moves touch the heart of Mother Earth and Father Heaven. As they dance they fall on the ground. They lose their balance because of the dance rigors and extreme hunger from fasting. Thanks be to God, the men are there to catch them when "the spirit knocks them down." When they wake up from fainting in the spirit, they find nothing has changed. Their problems have not gone away but their sadness has been replaced by some joy—even if it is temporary. They will still need to attend to their problems. But they need to be distracted from thinking about them for a while because they have become overwhelming. These African women have been maimed psychologically by suffering. They have become extremely weak. They can no longer face the deeply disturbing issues in their cultures and societies. They need to be distracted. The situation is becoming hopeless and these women are helpless. At least they get some temporary relief and happiness. They dance like goddesses. They want to shake off their misery and sorrow. It is free for all. They call it tarry night. Some call it a crusade.*

The crusades are like a soothing ointment on the wound. But the wound is becoming deep and painful.

147

Soon the ointment may no longer cover it. Pentecostalism and spiritual churches have swept African Christians off their feet and are rapidly replacing the authentic Christian faith described in the Acts of the Apostles. I use Pentecostalism and spiritual churches to describe the twenty-first-century evangelism. It is revivalism. It is marked by robust and loud forms of worship filled with songs, music, and outbursts of overt behaviors claimed to be manifestations of different inner stirrings. Most of such gatherings are either in a church building or in an open space. Different terms are used to describe these gatherings, such as tarry nights, fellowships, or crusades. It is flowery, exciting, and even fun. It is more appealing to the present generation of Africans. It provides physical as well as emotional exercises with a temporary spiritual flavor. A visit to a Christian night crusade or mass fellowship is needed to understand the phenomenon. You may be forced to think that Africans do miss the moonlight game.

Recreation and Religion: The moonlight game is a traditional evening recreation for youth still practiced in some places. "Onwa tibe, ije aguba agadi"—"the crippled elders long to walk again when the moon is out"—is a proverb that describes how much the elders miss youthful age. The present day forms of night worship provide adequately what were lost in the areas of African evening recreations. "Young men and women should not go out at night," the first missionaries said. "They might fall to temptations and commit sins of impurity." But sacredness was maintained during the moonlight games before the missionaries arrived. The young men stayed on their part of the village square while the young women stayed on theirs. But each group was not too distant from the other. This was for protection and help in case of emergency. This customary recreation has been effaced from many African societies, particularly in urban areas. Some people deem it pagan and uncivilized to call for moonlight games. Nowadays it is okay to go to a moonlight (even if it means artificially creating the moon by electricity) game but have you call it a Christian crusade or tarry night. Funny but true!

Do these crusades exhibit the gifts of the Holy Spirit— wisdom, knowledge, understanding, counsel, fortitude, piety, and fear of God? Answer the question yourself after attending a crusade in a rural area of any African country.

It took a long time before I agreed to attend a crusade. I attended crusades in several countries before I decided on a name for the movement: effervescent church. Could this effervescent church be a reminiscent of what was lost, namely traditional evening recreations? Could this be what attracts so many to the crusade grounds? But the men do not flock there like the women do. Do women need this type of religion more than men? Could it be that recreational needs have changed? There are large crowds at these crusades. Whether they are Baptists, Catholics, Evangelicals, or Pentecostals the story is the same. In recent times some of these crusades have become more ecumenical. All are welcome to bring their problem. African traditional religion (ATR) believers are commonly found at Christian crusades.

African women seem to need recreation in the evening more than men do. They need a place where they could bear their sorrows without having to tell an elaborate story about them. When it is time to give testimony they can skip the ugly part and share the good things God has done for them. Like a woman who has given birth, no one remembers the birth pangs or talks about the agony of being in labor. For some it might have started with abuse of some sort. But only the happy ending is shared. The crusade has become many African women's getaway. Some claim it is also a spiritual rejuvenation for them. For others it is a break from the abuse and chain of discrimination in their marriage and family life. In the crusade they find encouragement, energy, and strength to return home.

Dancing Away Our Troubles: At the end of an all-night vigil—singing, dancing, praying, visiting, socializing, casting out demons, and prophesying—she is ready to go back. She must return to her children. She would have loved "to dwell there" for the rest of her life. But her children need her. They need to hear her voice. They need to sit around her as she tells her story even though they don't quite understand. Sometimes she dances as she goes about her daily business. Her life is music to her children. Her body is so adaptable that its moves become dance steps as she does her daily chores. She needs to free herself of the burden of the heavy thoughts weighing on her. Her dancing is a way to shake off the rain of abuses from her husband, brothers, or in-laws. They melt in the melody of her angelic voice. She must sing them out and dance them off. She is a goddess. The stuff she is made of is known only to her Creator.

Who she is has been hidden from her so that she does not become proud. Humility is her garment and the perfume she wears. Those who come close to her experience her love, fortitude, and wisdom. She does not need people to tell her who she is. She knows, yet she remains humble. Some affirm, telling her how gifted she is. She responds, "If you belong to someone you can't claim to possess anything. The one who owns you possesses you and all you own." She is referring to the absolute sovereignty and power of the Creator.

Societal Expectations: Humility makes us flexible and adaptable. Nothing shocks a humble and simple person. When we expect to be placed on a certain level and treated accordingly our ego is hurt if these expectations are not met. We become upset. If we can we punish the culprit or the cause of our discontent. If we can't do this we don't associate with such a person or the cause of our feeling lower than we think we should be. No abuse seems to shock an African woman. I have heard humility described as "knowing who we are and accepting it." The task is in the "knowing." Most humans want to believe they are great, powerful, admirable, and popular. All these characteristics are defined by the people around us, and we feel we must fit their definition. People in any given society define the attributes and decide who has them. Having said this you may begin to realize as I do that there are more stars in our society than are acknowledged, just as there are more saints than are known. There are also more leaders than recognized and many more great people than acclaimed. We are gods and goddesses.

CHAPTER SIXTEEN
Colonization of the Mind

The most debilitating distraction for any human being is mental. Indeed, causing psychological misbalance is the best way to disable or defeat your enemy. We are susceptible to stress when our cognitive self become unbalanced. When this happens, our productivity level and success cannot be the same. Certain African cogno-traditional practices do more harm to the minds of women and children than the colonization era. Some of these practices may be tangential but their ripple effects are huge. Some are very serious cases.

In many African societies it is an abomination when a woman is caught cheating. It is almost taboo. But it seems to be okay for the man to have as many extramarital affairs as his brain and money can afford to cover his deeds. In the pre-Christian era, African men could marry as many wives as their resources allowed. One woman said to me, "All African dogs can eat human excrement, but only the dog that does not clean its mouth is called a shit eater. My husband is a dog. Recently he started bringing his mistresses to our matrimonial bed—but the shame is his." Asked if she is concerned about contracting venereal diseases or HIV/AIDS, she responded, "My God will continue to protect me." I looked into her eyes and said "Amen" to her act of faith. She may know that her faith won't protect her from HIV/AIDS, but what does she do? Her only recourse is tenacious belief in

OGHENE. Some husbands, with the help of their families abuse their wives. These abused women have no system or structure to turn to for help. In the pre-modernization past, kindred and communities would intervene in severe cases. These clan and kindred resources have become porous and fluid. Urban migration and the search for white-collar jobs have introduced less bonding in African societies than in the past.

Any culture has the tendency and power to colonize its citizens. When negative behaviors such as biases, profiling, and prejudices become a way of life the people in that culture become controlled by these behaviors. Profiling, marginalization, and labeling are forms of stereotyping that do great harm. These social ills are becoming more and more prevalent in African societies. Love, community, and impersonal lifestyles that used to be present among African people are disappearing. Individualism is creeping in faster. Yet African systems and structures do not have what it takes to benefit from the culture of individualism. Stereotyping and prejudice are diseases of the mind that afflict everyone, except the one with the disease. After a while those affected by the diseases begin to think they have them too. Some African women have internalized these abuses and victimizations to the point where it is scary. The example I gave above is an instance. If a typical rural African girl is raped, the first question generally asked of her is, "what did you go there to do". If a female student complains that a male teacher abuses her sexually, the listeners will say, "why not tell us the times you agreed". I don't get it. These injustices and abuses are so prevalent – sometimes obvious and some other times subtle. There is no protection or accountability whatsoever. You even see some women mete it out to the children and other women. For example madams abuse their house-helps. *One day in 1980, one woman on our street in Owerri beat her house-help until neighbors intervened. After everyone left she beat the girl harder until she passed out. When the girl awoke she ran away from the madam. In the morning she was found dead under a parked car on the street. The madam was freely moving about. People mouthed at her, called her all sorts of abusive names but no one charged her. All she did was move out from our street when she became uncomfortable with the name-calling. This woman was an active member of Christian women group.*

In this millennium, when African Christianity can be said to be very flowery and growing, I want to think that what sustains the boom are the poverty and ignorance of many of my people. It is easy to control and indoctrinate them. When the wind blows high, the leaves will fall and the plants will be naked. The fear is that "the butts of the chicken might be exposed" when that mighty wind begins to blow in the African Church.

Following is a true story that occurred in an all-girls' boarding school in Africa.

The incident took place in a junior high school in 1999. Looking back I would like to say that the devil must have been out of its chains that year to try his last tricks on God's children. Our reasoning was frozen by the white-dominance and white-superiority in the school. It started like a no-big-deal incident but escalated to a point of being a crime. The school principal (a missionary American nun) had threatened the students that if they did not find their misplaced dormitory key, they would not be allowed out of their dormitory. The students said their night prayers and went to bed about 9:00 PM. In the morning they had not found their key and so remained locked in the dormitory until 11:00 AM. I was very disturbed. I confronted the nun-principal. I asked her if she would do that in her home country without going to jail. I knew I was risking my vocation but I did not care. I wanted justice and fairness. I wanted respect for those students. I wanted their dignity upheld and their womanhood appreciated.

155

Some of the students were menstruating. They had used their buckets and bowls for toilets and bathroom needs. Passing the dormitory, it was stinking. I could not stand it. I went to the principal's office and was told she had gone to town. The bell for angelus tolled. (In Catholic institutions, it is common to have the bell toll at 6:00am, 12noon and 6:00pm for Marian prayers called angelus) *I stood there and asked the Blessed Mother of Jesus to give me the strength I needed to confront this horrible evil. I prayed for wisdom. I prayed most importantly for enough peace and justice in my heart to propel me to do the right thing.*

I approached the school carpenter, who told me he had a spare key. He made me swear I would not tell the school principal he gave me the key. I obliged. I let the students out. Fighting back tears I helped them—more than twenty girls—use the bathroom and toilets outside their dormitory. They cleaned themselves and the buckets, bowls, and containers they used for their bathroom and toilet needs. They showered and I took them back to their dormitory. The dormitory was locked again and the key given back to the carpenter. The students sat on their beds to wait for the principal. I went to my room, threw myself on my bed, and wept bitterly. From that day, I refused to shut up my mouth whenever I observed any form of injustice or abuse in the school. I was constantly in trouble for speaking out. The woman in me had become stronger and bolder. You can anticipate what happened to me. A year later I was fired. I cried but it did not break me. It was not the first time I hit the rock.

People—foreigners, missionaries, and indigenes—do many obnoxious things in Africa. Many of these things are crimes according to human rights standards. Yet no one holds them accountable. I want to believe it is because they have colonized our thinking faculties and brainwashed our reasoning abilities. Oppression and abuse seem to go in circles: men to women, women to self, other women and children, children to self, fellow children and parents. This vicious circle seems to cripple the community. Some psychologists call it internalized oppression. This is way beyond any psychological naming

Certain belief structures have formed in the cognitive templates of many African women. They have accepted their role as child-bearer and taking care of husbands. How can anybody accept that their sex *is* their vocation? This is ridiculous. It is like being told you are a man and therefore that is your vocation. Childbearing is part and parcel of womanhood. Only a woman can conceive and bear a child. Accordingly, African women have been made to believe this is their vocation, the same way they have been made to believe they are natural recipients of injustice and abuse. You may have heard it said that African women are called the Mother Earth so that men can sit on them. There are even more demeaning and obnoxious things African women are made to believe about themselves. Some of these are simply damaging while others are violations of their human rights. Believing these things has become part of some African women's identity.

An African woman understands her world and culture as a way of life. However, some of these cultural and traditional beliefs are neither life-giving nor life-sustaining. Her perception of her roles as a girl, woman, sister, mother, wife, and widow are defined within her cultural template. If her culture is victimizing or oppressive she perceives her role and position as the natural recipient. In my view, this goes way beyond the so-called learned helplessness. For instance, they are made to believe they can't compete with men in high stakes entrepreneurship.

When you visit hot business spots in Africa like Nnewi in Nigeria or Kumasi in Ghana, you will count more men entrepreneurs than women in serious business enterprises. You rarely see women in top government positions. But you see more women than men in the church. In the same church, most decision-making positions are occupied by men. These things need not be this way. With recent movements and western education, things are beginning to change. But there is a long way to go.

Mama Sophia posing for joy of liberation

The Final Baton: An African woman is beginning to understand that the baton has been handed over to her. She has started to learn the use of numbers and philosophy in order to communicate well with men. Men think she is still not very good at it. Some still think she is a dummy. That is why they exclude her from many positions. But she is *universe* in herself. Heaven and earth have united to build a home in her. Because she is a goddess there is a bouquet of flowers in her being while she herself is a flower in the *uni-vase*. The difference between a man and a woman is *the difference*. As always said by experts of multiculturalism, "differences do not mean deficiencies" Our difference is the one thing we share in common. Our differences form the bouquet of flowers in our uni-vase. The African woman does not stand out, yet her presence brings an aroma of consolation and an elegance of beauty to the bouquet. That bouquet is not the same without her presence and contributions.

How do we help her appreciate her unique presence in the formation of the bouquet? Above all she should be educated. Then she in turn will educate her nation. When all have been educated—women as well as men—it will be easier for him to see what was unfair in the past. He will begin to appreciate her struggles. Together they will benefit from the strength that has carried her through. Together they will harness the power of their authority for the development of the land—and their children will be great.

A Brief Bio of Ngozi T. Udoye, IHJ, PhD
President and Cofounder of AfWiAm

Ngozi, popularly known as NG, is an Igbo woman from Igbo-Ukwu, the ancient city in Eastern Nigeria where bronze and other archeological treasures were discovered. She refers to herself as the child of the world village. NG has emerged as a brilliant scholar and author. She graduated summa cum laude from the University of Nigeria Nsukka, receiving the Indira Gandhi award as the most outstanding female graduates in 1998. She has taken up the challenge of working with and for African women and children. She joins other women to make this mission a reality. NG migrated to United States in 2003 in her search for safety, emancipation, liberation and empowerment. She is a motivational speaker, an international educator and a human rights activist for women and children.

NG received her masters' degrees and doctorate from Loyola University Chicago. She loves and enjoys learning, hence she calls herself "Sophia." She loves to see others develop and become their best. Accordingly, she spends time motivating and helping others, especially women and girls. She helps them develop their self-empowering abilities. NG developed and uses the program of Critical Thinking and Internal Balance (CTIB) as a tool in her mission with African women. She believes women have enormous potential but certain socio-cultural and cogno-traditional practices prevent them from becoming their best.

Ng and many other African women *believe the salvation of Africa lies in the hands of women,* and together they will lead Africa's children to the promised land where freedom, justice, and equality will reign.

About the Cover Illustration

The cover image is an attempt to depict the symbolic beauty and immeasurable depth of the womanhood.
Artist: Philippe Gibson
Email: info@afwiam.org

On behalf of African women and children, AfWiAm will like to thank you for purchasing this book. The proceeds go to assist the mission of African Women in America.
Website: www.afwiam.org

For Group Discussions and Book Club

1. What's your opinion about non-profit organizations in Africa?
2. Have you visited Africa? Please share your thoughts about perceived or observed economic and political roles of women.
3. African women are the major participants in liberation efforts for Africa. What is your opinion about this statement?
4. If you have one message for the African women, what would it be?
5. Would you like to sponsor an African woman/child or project? Choose your preferred country, and contact Stephany Toman. Email: secretary@afwiam.org

For further inquiries, please contact Afia Ohemeng. Email: info@afwiam.org

Would you like your thoughts and opinion to be part of AfWiAm decision? Please send your contributions to: president@afwiam.org

LaVergne, TN USA
10 September 2010

196507LV00003B/9/P